Rethinking
New Testament
TEXTUAL
CRITICISM

Rethinking
New Testament
TEXTUAL
CRITICISM

Edited by
David Alan Black

Baker Academic

A Division of Baker Book House Co
Grand Rapids, Michigan 49516

Published by Baker Academic
a division of Baker Book House Company
P.O. Box 6287, Grand Rapids, MI 49516-6287

Printed in the United States of America

Library of Congress Cataloging-in-Publication Data

Rethinking New Testament textual criticism / edited by David Alan Black.
    p.   cm.
    Includes bibliographical references and indexes.
    ISBN 0-8010-2280-0 (pbk.)
    1. Bible. N.T.—Criticism, Textual—Congresses. I. Black, David Alan, 1952–
BS2325 .R48 2002
225.4'86—dc21   2002018317

For information about Baker Academic, visit our web site:
www.bakeracademic.com

To the New Testament faculties
of the Universities of Oxford and Leeds
for extending to me the privilege
of lecturing to their students,
November 2000

CONTENTS

ABBREVIATIONS

Editions of the Greek New Testament

NA   general reference to the Nestle-Aland series of Greek New Testaments

NA²⁵   E. Nestle and K. Aland, eds., *Novum Testamentum Graece* (25th ed.; Stuttgart: Württembergische Bibelanstalt, 1963)

NA²⁶   K. Aland and B. Aland, eds., *Novum Testamentum Graece* (26th ed.; Stuttgart: Deutsche Bibelstiftung, 1979)

NA²⁷   B. Aland, K. Aland, J. Karavidopoulos, C. M. Martini, and B. M. Metzger, eds., *Novum Testamentum Graece* (27th ed.; Stuttgart: Deutsche Bibelgesellschaft, 1993)

RP   M. A. Robinson and W. G. Pierpont, *The New Testament in the Original Greek according to the Byzantine/Majority Textform* (Atlanta: Original Word, 1991)

UBS   general reference to the United Bible Societies series of Greek New Testaments

UBS¹   K. Aland, M. Black, C. M. Martini, B. M. Metzger, and A. Wikgren, eds., *The Greek New Testament* (1st ed.; New York: United Bible Societies, 1966)

UBS²   K. Aland, M. Black, C. M. Martini, B. M. Metzger, and A. Wikgren, eds., *The Greek New Testament* (2d ed.; New York: United Bible Societies, 1968)

UBS³   K. Aland, M. Black, C. M. Martini, B. M. Metzger, and A. Wikgren, eds., *The Greek New Testament* (3d ed.; New York: United Bible Societies, 1975; 3d corrected ed. in 1983)

UBS⁴   B. Aland, K. Aland, J. Karavidopoulos, C. M. Martini, and B. M. Metzger, eds., *The Greek New Testament* (4th ed.; Stuttgart: Deutsche Bibelgesellschaft/United Bible Societies, 1993)

WH   B. F. Westcott and F. J. A. Hort, *The New Testament in the Original Greek* (2 vols.; London: Macmillan, 1881–82 [2d ed. of vol. 2 in 1896])

Bibliographic

P.Oxy. *The Oxyrhynchus Papyri* (67 vols. to date; Graeco-Roman Memoirs; London: Egypt Exploration Society for the British Academy, 1898–)

STM   E. J. Epp and G. D. Fee, *Studies in the Theory and Method of New Testament Textual Criticism* (Studies and Documents 45; Grand Rapids: Eerdmans, 1993)

TCGNT   B. M. Metzger, *A Textual Commentary on the Greek New Testament: A Companion Volume to the United Bible Societies' Greek New Testament (Fourth Revised Edition)* (2d ed.; Stuttgart: Deutsche Bibelgesellschaft, 1994 [1st ed. in 1971; corrected ed. in 1975])

TNTCR   B. D. Ehrman and M. W. Holmes, eds., *The Text of the New Testament in Contemporary Research: Essays on the Status Quaestionis: A Volume in Honor of Bruce M. Metzger* (Studies and Documents 46; Grand Rapids: Eerdmans, 1995)

INTRODUCTION

DAVID ALAN BLACK

Should I take a course in textual criticism?" I am often asked this question by Greek students who already feel unduly pressed by paradigms and principal parts in their grammar classes. To many of them it seems that learning the language of the New Testament is challenging enough without the added burden of trying to understand what is written at the bottom of the pages in their Greek New Testaments, which itself seems akin to a foreign language. If mastering Greek grammar is the goal, it appears irrelevant indeed that one should dabble in a science that even the experts cannot seem to agree on.

Years ago I, too, debated in college whether to study textual criticism, but when a course on that subject was offered I could not resist the temptation to enroll. The year was 1975, and the professor was Harry Sturz, head of the Greek Department at Biola University, who earlier had written his doctoral dissertation at Grace Seminary on the topic of the Byzantine text. Despite some tedious moments in the course (such as collating Greek manuscripts—a forgotten discipline today), I found the subject of textual criticism fascinating, not least because the professor espoused a position that seemed to fly in the face of the accepted thinking of the day. We read and used all the standard works on the subject—Tischendorf, von Soden, Westcott and Hort, Metzger, and others—and were required to resolve a textual problem on our own, using a template the professor had designed to help us work through both the external and internal evidence. I left the class with an appreciably better understanding of those hieroglyphics at the bottom of my Greek New Testament, as well as with an eagerness to further my textual studies. After graduation, Dr. Sturz hired me to teach Greek at Biola University while I attended Talbot Seminary, where I elected to major in New Testament. Still fascinated by the subject of textual criticism, I wrote my master's thesis on the variant reading in Ephesians 1:1—a highly debated text involving the words ἐν Ἐφέσῳ. The conclusions of my thesis were published in an essay entitled "The Peculiarities of Ephesians and the Ephesian Address,"[1] in which I sought to defend the originality of ἐν Ἐφέσῳ and the traditional Ephesian destination (even though this was, and still is, a minority view among New Testament scholars). Graduation from Talbot saw me at the University of Basel in Switzerland studying for my doctorate under Swedish New Testament scholar Bo Reicke. My Basel dissertation took me deeper into Pauline theology and exegesis, with not a few text-critical problems to deal with along the way.[2] Trying to resolve such problems only confirmed my view that textual criticism is a discipline with much to commend itself to other fields of study.

During and after my sojourn in Basel, I had the opportunity to evaluate several textual problems in the Gospels. In later publications I suggested that a number of Byzantine readings that have not found their way into the text of modern critical editions need to be given a hearing.[3] I also called into question what I viewed as a dangerous trend in Gospel studies in general and Matthean studies in particular—the tendency to resort to conjectural emendation, even when the text yielded perfectly good sense.[4] Later

1. D. A. Black, "The Peculiarities of Ephesians and the Ephesian Address," Grace Theological Journal 2 (1981): 59–73.
2. D. A. Black, Paul, Apostle of Weakness: Astheneia and Its Cognates in the Pauline Epistles (Bern: Lang, 1984).
3. D. A. Black, "The Text of John 3:13," Grace Theological Journal 6 (1985): 49–66; idem, "Jesus on Anger: The Text of Matthew 5:22a Revisited," Novum Testamentum 30 (1988): 1–8; idem, "The Text of Mark 6:20," New Testament Studies 34 (1988): 141–45.
4. D. A. Black, "Conjectural Emendations in the Gospel of Matthew," Novum Testamentum 31 (1989): 1–15.

still, I produced a brief introduction to textual criticism designed mainly for pastors and lay people, many of whom were interested in the so-called King James Version debate. In *New Testament Textual Criticism: A Concise Guide* I discussed in simple terms the art and science of textual criticism, its history and materials, and the current debate over methodology.[5] Recalling my own experience as a Greek student, I have used this book in my beginning Greek classes to introduce students to the relevance of textual studies for exegesis and preaching and to prepare them for future studies using Metzger's *Text of the New Testament*.

When I arrived in North Carolina to take up my current teaching post at Southeastern Seminary, I quickly became aware that the text of the New Testament was a lively topic of discussion on campus. Some students were outspoken advocates of the *textus receptus* and the King James Version, while others were equally supportive of modern critical texts such as the United Bible Societies' *Greek New Testament*. In addition, one of my colleagues on the New Testament faculty, Maurice Robinson, whose doctoral work had been in textual criticism, had himself spent years developing the Byzantine-priority view, and in the course of dialoging with him I became aware that here was an articulate scholar whose defense of the Byzantine text seemed both cogent and compelling. Would it not be useful, I mused, if we could assemble in Wake Forest leading proponents of the various text-critical positions and let them present their views so that students and faculty alike could make up their own minds?

With President Paige Patterson's enthusiastic support, I assembled a committee to organize a New Testament symposium on our campus. I would be responsible for contacting prospective participants and for arranging the program, while my colleague David Beck would handle the on-campus arrangements. No expense was to be spared in making our guests feel welcome. The visiting scholars would be housed in our comfortable guest cottages (the Manor and Lyon Houses), and meals would be taken at Magnolia Hill, the president's home. The speakers would be met personally at the airport and shuttled to and from campus. Finally, the campus bookstore would set up a special

5. D. A. Black, *New Testament Textual Criticism: A Concise Guide* (Grand Rapids: Baker, 1994).

display of the participants' publications for sale in the foyer of Binkley Chapel, the venue for the symposium.

Thus it was that on April 6–7, 2000, some of the world's leading experts in the field of New Testament studies arrived on the campus of Southeastern Seminary to read papers and to engage in dialog with their colleagues. The conference, entitled "Symposium on New Testament Studies: A Time for Reappraisal," was designed to expose students and other interested parties to the main positions held by New Testament scholars in three debated areas of research: the Synoptic problem, the authorship of Hebrews, and New Testament textual criticism. Each seminar included a keynote address laying out in broad terms the *status quaestionis* in the area under debate, three main papers, a response, and a panel discussion.

The seminar on textual criticism included papers by influential scholars who have shaped New Testament text-critical studies over the past decades. In his keynote address, Eldon Jay Epp introduced the audience to contemporary approaches to textual criticism and provided an assessment of the state of the discipline as well as a perspective for understanding current and future issues.

Michael Holmes presented the case for reasoned eclecticism in textual criticism. Holmes, who represents the majority of practicing textual critics and editors of scholarly editions in the past thirty years or so, succinctly described an approach in which a reading that has a good range of manuscript support and that seems to have been the cause for the secondary readings is to be preferred.

J. K. Elliott presented the case for thoroughgoing eclecticism. Elliott is identified with an approach to textual criticism that accepts as original a reading that can be defended on the grounds of internal evidence (language, style, usage, author's theology, etc.). This approach pays scant attention to the number and alleged weight of the manuscripts supporting a reading. In theory, thoroughgoing eclecticism is prepared to print a reading supported by only a few (possibly late) manuscripts if that reading can be justified on internal grounds. This method stemmed largely from C. H. Turner's famous "Notes" on Markan usage published in the 1920s and was popularized by George D. Kilpatrick.

Maurice Robinson offered a case for Byzantine priority and what he believes to be a viable theory of textual transmission.

Discounting the genealogical method and mere numerical "nose-counting," he defended the Textform that predominated throughout the greatest period of manuscript copying of the Greek New Testament (ca. 350–1516 C.E.). To wrap things up, Moisés Silva read his response to his colleagues' papers, employing a good deal of wit and humor, much to the delight of the audience. The panel discussion that ensued allowed the audience to pose questions to the scholars and gave the scholars themselves an opportunity to engage in further dialog.

The reaction to the Southeastern symposium was enthusiastic, with over four hundred registered guests in attendance for some or all of the papers. It is now my pleasure to make the papers on textual criticism available to the reading public. Deep appreciation goes to each person who has been involved in the planning and production of this volume, especially to the authors themselves. Additional thanks are extended to David Beck of the New Testament faculty of Southeastern Seminary for his support and assistance, to my research assistants Chris Thompson and Andrew Neamtu for cheerfully attending to a myriad of details, to my secretary Phyllis Keith for her assistance with correspondence, to Davidson Press for underwriting a portion of the symposium expenses, to Jim Kinney and his staff at Baker Academic for readying the papers for publication, and to President Patterson and Dean Russ Bush for their support of the project from its inception.

It is my hope that this volume will succeed in both surveying and evaluating the present state of text-critical studies in the United States and beyond. As Epp aptly states elsewhere, "New Testament textual criticism is a vigorous and stimulating discipline, in which—as history demonstrates—new discoveries are always possible (though not assured) and in which many theoretical decisions—fundamental to the discipline—remain to be made on the basis of the materials we have."[6] There is, therefore, much that students can learn from reading a book on textual criticism. Perhaps, too, this volume will help fledgling Greek students answer the question with which this introduction opened with a resounding "yes!"

6. E. J. Epp, "Textual Criticism," in *The New Testament and Its Modern Interpreters* (ed. E. J. Epp and G. W. MacRae; Philadelphia: Fortress/Atlanta: Scholars Press, 1989), 106 (= *STM* 44).

1

ISSUES IN NEW TESTAMENT TEXTUAL CRITICISM

*Moving from the Nineteenth Century
to the Twenty-First Century*

ELDON JAY EPP

I begin with a textual variant, though not from the New Testament.[1] For many years I kept on a note card—and in my mind—a couplet that has guided my own work, for it describes a common weakness of interpreters that I was determined to avoid. It read:

> Exegetes who major issues shun
> And hold their farthing candles to the sun.

My scribbled note said that this was from Alexander Pope (1688–1744), and when I decided to quote it here, I consulted

1. This essay covers vast portions of the New Testament text-critical discipline. To avoid an even lengthier set of footnotes, the reader is often pointed to my earlier writings where detailed discussions can be found with full references. This is done with apologies to researchers whose works are bypassed in the present essay, though fully acknowledged in those earlier publications.

a complete concordance of Pope's poetry. I was unable, however, to confirm the reference, so I put a footnote in the preliminary version of the essay saying I had been unsuccessful in locating its source. Almost immediately, J. K. Elliott sent an email message, kindly informing me that my quotation obviously was a textual variant (probably by way of oral tradition) of the following couplet by Edward Young (1683–1765), whose life overlapped that of Pope for fifty-seven years; it reads:

> How commentators each dark passage shun
> And hold their farthing candle to the sun.

The former reading had considerable influence on me, yet it now appears to be a variant of the latter that has been altered in the process of transmission. Therefore, in the face of these two variant readings, I decided to follow a line of interpretation that I shall describe near the end of this essay, namely, adopt both readings and pronounce that textual critics will do well (a) if they do not try to avoid dark, difficult passages and (b) if they stick to major issues. Both actions will prevent the light they cast on the New Testament text from being obliterated by the sunshine of the great textual critics that have gone before.

In what follows, I hope to sketch several major issues facing the discipline at this fascinating point in its history. Some may be rather familiar, traditional issues, while others will offer new challenges well beyond the familiar. If we are to move further toward resolution, some issues will require continued labors on long-standing and well-defined tasks, while others not only will demand accommodation to radical new ideas but also are likely to generate resistance among those who may view them as paths too risky to follow.

As an instructive framework for our considerations, I shall identify several issues facing New Testament textual criticism at the outset of the twenty-first century and then compare them with the same or similar issues in the nineteenth century. More specifically, I shall describe, first, the status of each issue at the end or perhaps in the latter half of the nineteenth century, a period of significant progress in discovering and analyzing manuscripts, in addressing principles for approving or disapproving variant readings, and in creating widely accepted critical editions of the Greek New Testament text. Second, after tracing progress during the twentieth century, each issue's present status will be assessed, followed by suggestions about where the discipline might be headed in the year 2000 and beyond. Incidentally, merely postulating this particular framework implies at the outset that the issues in textual criticism have not changed markedly during the past century, and, indeed, to a large extent this is the case, since some issues remain largely or partially unresolved and we have learned to live with compromises. At the same time, however, with the entire twentieth century now in view, we can see the prodigious labors expended in analyzing the numerous and notably early manuscripts that came to light during that period and in the development of theories, tools, and methods for studying the transmission, history, and nature of the New Testament text—including some radical new approaches and attitudes.[2] So, the trick is to determine how our successes or failures during the twentieth century position us now to move forward decisively in this new century.

I propose to identify five issues currently requiring attention, though some will have to be treated in cursory fashion due to space limitations. I begin with a truism: Since New Testament textual criticism is both an art and a science, as a discipline it is all about *choice* and *decision*. I therefore characterize the major issues as follows:

1. *Choosing among **variants**—and deciding on **priority**.* This is the issue of the so-called canons of criticism— what are the arguments we employ to decide between the variant readings in a given variation unit, and, as a

2. This may appear to be contradictory to my Hatch Memorial Lecture delivered at the 1973 Annual Meeting of the Society of Biblical Literature in Chicago ("The Twentieth-Century Interlude in New Testament Textual Criticism," *Journal of Biblical Literature* 93 [1974]: 386–414 [= *STM* 83–108]), but a quarter century has passed, and, as the following discussions show, progress has been made in numerous respects. I now find myself in agreement, therefore, with the more optimistic outlook in L. W. Hurtado, "Beyond the Interlude? Developments and Directions in New Testament Textual Criticism," in *Studies in the Early Text of the Gospels and Acts: The Papers of the First Birmingham Colloquium on the Textual Criticism of the New Testament* (ed. D. G. K. Taylor; Texts and Studies 3/1; Birmingham, England: University of Birmingham Press, 1999), 26–49.

consequence, how do we put it all together to reconstruct readings that make up a text most like that of the
early Christian community?

2. *Choosing among **manuscripts**—and deciding on **groups**.*
Here the concern is text-types—can we isolate clusters
of manuscripts that constitute distinguishable kinds of
texts as evidenced by shared textual characteristics? And
can we marshal these to sketch the history of the New
Testament text?

3. *Choosing among **critical editions**—and deciding for
compromise.* Do our current critical editions of the
Greek New Testament reflect a reasonable approximation to the text (or a text) that was extant in very early
Christianity? The difficulties inherent in reconstructing
such a text suggest that compromise may be the order of
the day.

4. *Choosing to address **context**—and deciding on **influence**.*
This engages the issue of placing manuscripts and variant readings in their church-historical, cultural, and
intellectual contexts—how did they influence the church
and its theology, and how, in turn, did the church and
the surrounding culture influence the manuscripts and
their variant readings?

5. *Choosing to address **goals and directions**—and deciding
on **meanings and approaches**.* What is the goal or what
are the goals of New Testament textual criticism? More
specifically, what *do* we mean by original text and what
can we mean by it? And how will our decisions inform
our future directions and our methods?

Obviously, this is a tall order for a single essay, and at point
after point we shall have to be content with broad strokes on a
very large canvas (and tolerate numerous footnotes).

Choosing among Variants—and Deciding on Priority:
The Issue of the Canons of Criticism

Utilizing canons of criticism, that is, rules or principles to
judge the quality and priority of competing variant readings in

New Testament manuscripts, goes back at least as far as Irenaeus (second century), Origen (third century), and Jerome
(fourth and early fifth centuries), who on occasion discuss the
age or nature of manuscripts or explain why they prefer one
reading over another. As examples, Irenaeus prefers a reading in
the Apocalypse 13:18 "found in all the good [or weighty] and ancient copies," and Origen rejects the reading Jesus prefixed to
Barabbas in Matthew 27:16–17 both because "in many copies" it
is not present and because the name Jesus would not be used of
evildoers.[3]

The modern formulation and discussion of criteria for judging variants accelerated from the list of forty-three drawn up
by Gerhard von Mastricht in 1711 to Richard Bentley's *Proposals for Printing a New Edition* [of a Greek and Latin New Testa-
ment] in 1720, to the increasingly influential canons of J. A.
Bengel (1725), J. J. Wettstein (1730 and 1751–52), J. J. Griesbach (1796–1806), and Karl Lachmann (1831–1850).[4] Noteworthy from this period is Bentley's insistence on using "the
most ancient and venerable MSS. in Greek and Roman capital
letters," whose readings are to be confirmed by the old versions and fathers "within the first five centuries," because
"what has crept into any copies since is of no value or author-

3. B. M. Metzger, "The Practice of Textual Criticism among the Church Fathers," in *Studia Patristica 12* (ed. E. A. Livingstone; Texte und Untersuchun-
gen 115; Berlin: Akademie-Verlag, 1975), 1:340–41 (on Irenaeus, *Against
Heresies* 5.30.1) and 1:342 (on Origen, *Commentary on Matthew* 121 [GCS 38 =
Origenes Werke 11:255, 24–31 Klostermann]). See also K. K. Hulley, "Principles
of Textual Criticism Known to St. Jerome," *Harvard Studies in Classical Philology* 55 (1944): 87–109; B. M. Metzger, "Explicit References in the Works of Origen to Variant Readings in New Testament Manuscripts," in *Biblical and
Patristic Studies in Memory of Robert Pierce Casey* (ed. J. N. Birdsall and R. W.
Thomson; Freiburg: Herder, 1963), 78–95 (repr. in Metzger's *Historical and Literary Studies: Pagan, Jewish, and Christian* [New Testament Tools and Studies
8; Leiden: Brill, 1968], 88–103); idem, "St. Jerome's Explicit References to
Variant Readings in Manuscripts of the New Testament," in *Text and Interpretation: Studies in the New Testament Presented to Matthew Black* (ed. E. Best
and R. McL. Wilson; Cambridge: Cambridge University Press, 1979), 179–90
(repr. in Metzger's *New Testament Studies: Philological, Versional, and Patristic*
[New Testament Tools and Studies 10; Leiden: Brill, 1980], 199–210).
4. These are discussed in considerable detail in E. J. Epp, "The Eclectic
Method in New Testament Textual Criticism: Solution or Symptom?" *Harvard
Theological Review* 69 (1976): 217–29 (= STM 144–55).

ity."[5] Noteworthy also are Bengel's celebrated principle that "the harder reading is to be preferred"[6] and his reliance on the oldest Greek manuscripts and the geographical distribution of witnesses. In addition, Bengel was the first to enunciate the influential affirmation that textual witnesses must be *weighed and not merely counted*.[7] Wettstein reaffirmed most of these criteria in 1730, stating also his preference for the shorter reading and for the reading in conformity with the author's style, though not necessarily preferring the more orthodox reading. Wettstein, however, had abandoned this general approach by the time his 1751–52 edition appeared, having convinced himself that the oldest Greek manuscripts had been corrupted by those in Latin—not a defensible view. Then, Griesbach reinforced and refined Bengel's criterion of preferring the harder reading, and, like Wettstein, he also favored the shorter reading (the first criterion in his list, though stated with numerous qualifications); however, again like Wettstein, Griesbach was suspicious of readings that supported piety or suited orthodox theology. In addition, Griesbach clearly favored the ancient witnesses, as did Lachmann after him. Indeed, it was the latter who afforded the "received text" of the sixteenth century no authority, thus effecting a decisive break with the *textus receptus*, until then the standard critical text of the New Testament.[8]

In the mid- to late nineteenth century, however, these canons of criticism came into their own in the hands of Constantin von Tischendorf (1849), S. P. Tregelles (1854), and B. F. Westcott and F. J. A. Hort (1881–82). Tischendorf and Tregelles provided straightforward principles, while those employed by WH must be extracted and systematized from Hort's detailed discussions.

5. For Bentley's text, see A. A. Ellis, ed., *Bentleii critica sacra: Notes on the Greek and Latin Text of the New Testament, Extracted from the Bentley MSS. in Trinity College Library, with the Abbé Rulotta's Collation of the Vatican Codex B, a Specimen of Bentley's Intended Edition, and an Account of His Collations* (Cambridge: Deighton, Bell, 1862), xvii–xix.

6. Bengel phrased it *proclivi scriptioni praestat ardua*, though it is more commonly expressed as *difficilior lectio potior*; see Epp, "Eclectic Method," 220 (= *STM* 146–47).

7. Ibid., 220–22 (= *STM* 147–48).

8. For detail on Griesbach and Lachmann, see ibid., 225–31 (= *STM* 150–55).

Overall, the result was extensive agreement among the three approaches.[9] Tischendorf, for example, stressed that "the text should be sought solely from ancient witnesses" and, echoing Lachmann, that the resulting authority of the oldest Greek codices is not "surmounted by the disagreement of most or even of all the recent codices."[10] He also gave preference to "the reading that appears to have occasioned the other readings," which he describes as the basic rule.[11] Tregelles, in turn, emphasized "the authority of ancient copies without allowing the 'received text' any prescriptive rights" and preferred the harder reading and the shorter reading.[12] Finally, as we near the end of the nineteenth century, WH exemplified all of the principles highlighted above, particularly its editors' preference for the older readings, manuscripts, or groups; for the reading that most aptly explains the existence of the others; for the harder (rather than the smoother) reading; and for "quality" readings rather than those with numerous supporting witnesses. In addition, WH preferred the single elements in a conflated reading, the reading best conforming to the author's style and grammar, and readings that are found in a manuscript that habitually contains superior readings, especially if such a manuscript is also an older one. As for the *textus receptus*, which they called the Syrian text, it is the farthest removed chronologically and qualitatively from the original text. Also, WH established a clear division between *external* and *internal* criteria,[13] an approach that will characterize all subsequent discussion of the canons of criticism. At the end of the nineteenth century, then, there was widespread agreement in the use of two differing sets of criteria, external and internal.

9. For discussion, see ibid., 231–42 (= *STM* 155–63).

10. This formulation was published in the second edition of Tischendorf's Greek New Testament (1849) and also quoted in the seventh edition (1859; pp. xxvii–xviii) and by C. R. Gregory in his prolegomena to Tischendorf's eighth edition (1896; 3:47–48).

11. See discussion in Epp, "Eclectic Method," 231–32 (= *STM* 155–56).

12. Ibid., 232–34 (= *STM* 156–57).

13. WH 2:19–39 (on internal evidence) and 2:39–66 (on external evidence, which WH call "genealogical evidence"). See discussion in Epp, "Eclectic Method," 234–42 (= *STM* 157–63). (In my abstracted list on 234–35 [= *STM* 157–58] of principles used by WH, I neglected to separate the external from the internal, though they are clearly distinguished by these editors.)

Before summarizing these categories, the term *criteria* deserves some thought. The Alands use the word *rules* ("Twelve Basic Rules [Grundregeln] for Textual Criticism") in their manual,[14] but they and all theorists and practitioners in the field know that these are not really rules that are or can be applied mechanically to decide priority among variants. On occasion, however, the criteria are misunderstood as functioning in that fashion,[15] for all the terms employed—"rules," "criteria," "principles," and the like—lend themselves to that kind of rigid interpretation. For a brief moment I considered a return to the old, perhaps obsolete term *canons* for these criteria, because *canon* refers to a measure; we might then call the criteria "measures" or "yardsticks" of priority, which we hold up to each variant to "take its measure" (as we say), even if that measure is not scientifically exact. Yet, the term *canon* more commonly implies a fixed and final measure, as in a limited collection of writings or a canonized saint. The criteria for priority, however, really are measures of *probability* or various complementary or even competing *arguments* for priority. Hence, we might use *probabilities*, a term drawn from Hort's phrases *transcriptional probabilities* and *intrinsic probabilities* (WH 2:20–22), which Bruce Metzger employed along with the term *criteria*.[16] Better, perhaps, is the simple term *arguments*, for arguments, after all, are of varying force, some more compelling and some less compelling, some more relevant and some less relevant, to a given situation or context, and arguments also can be used singly or in multiple,

14. K. Aland and B. Aland, *The Text of the New Testament: An Introduction to the Critical Editions and to the Theory and Practice of Modern Textual Criticism* (trans. E. F. Rhodes; 2d ed.; Grand Rapids: Eerdmans; Leiden: Brill, 1989), 280–81. They specifically reject a mechanical function for the rules on the harder reading, the shorter reading, and harmonization, as well as a mechanical following of a single manuscript or group of manuscripts (281).

15. For example, E. Tov thinks that such criteria are used mechanically by some in his field; he himself uses the term *rules* but rejects not only any mechanical application, but largely rejects the criteria themselves as too subjective to be practical; *Textual Criticism of the Hebrew Bible* (2d ed.; Minneapolis: Fortress/Assen: Van Gorcum, 2001), 302–10; see also the discussion below and nn. 30 and 43.

16. B. M. Metzger, *The Text of the New Testament: Its Transmission, Corruption, and Restoration* (3d ed.; New York: Oxford University Press, 1992), 209–10; idem, *TCGNT* 12*–13*.

complementary fashion. All of this fits very well the external and internal canons as they have developed historically and have been applied practically—and as they have been weakened or strengthened in efficacy during their utilization by textual criticism.

External arguments involve documentary factors—information about manuscripts and the history of their transmission—that is, the more clearly empirical data, such as the age and provenance of a manuscript in which a given reading is found, the age of a reading as ascertained by patristic support, the geographical range of a reading, and the identification of a manuscript's text-type and its place in the history of the New Testament text.[17] On the other hand, internal arguments relate to factors or characteristics *within* the text itself (over against the external data) and usually comprise a much longer list. Examples can be described in question form: Can this variant account for the rise of all the others in a variation unit? Does this variant conform to the writer's literary style, vocabulary, or theology? Is this variant harder than others, that is, rougher, less elegant, or less clear (though still making sense)? If the answer in these cases is "yes," the variant more probably should be accorded priority. Does a variant conform to/harmonize with a parallel passage (e.g., in another gospel), an Old Testament passage, liturgical forms or usage, or some extraneous item in the context? Does a variant show the influence of ideas from the later history or theology of the church? In these instances, if the answer is affirmative, the variant is more likely to be considered secondary or derivative. Also, can a variant be readily or plausibly explained as one of the usual, unintentional scribal errors? If so, we reverse the process and restore the probable reading of the scribe's exemplar.

Two internal arguments found in most lists are absent from the preceding summary: the Atticized-reading and the shorter-

---

17. My latest formulation of external and internal considerations is "Textual Criticism in the Exegesis of the New Testament, with an Excursus on Canon," in *Handbook to Exegesis of the New Testament* (ed. S. E. Porter; New Testament Tools and Studies 25; Leiden: Brill, 1997), 62–63 (internal) and 71–72 (external). Earlier formulations appeared in my "Eclectic Method," 243 (= *STM* 163–64); idem, "Textual Criticism (NT)," in *Anchor Bible Dictionary* (ed. D. N. Freedman et al.; New York: Doubleday, 1992), 6:431.

reading arguments; they require discussion, for they were seriously challenged during the twentieth century. In 1963 George D. Kilpatrick suggested that scribes in the second century tended to alter Koine Greek toward Attic Greek style, indicating that a reading should be discredited if it showed Atticist tendencies.[18] Subsequently, however, questions were raised about the efficacy of this argument on the grounds, among others, (a) that scribes in these cases may have had other intentions—other than moving toward Attic style—such as harmonization, and so on, and that Atticism, if it is assumed to have operated, had not functioned very well statistically;[19] (b) that some of the examples offered are not true Atticisms and that it is difficult in any case to assess Atticism before 400 C.E.;[20] or (c) that the scribal tendency may well have been to alter Attic Greek style to biblical (i.e., Septuagint) Greek rather than the other way around.[21] Kilpatrick and his pupil Keith El-

18. G. D. Kilpatrick, "Atticism and the Text of the Greek New Testament," in *Neutestamentliche Aufsätze: Festschrift für Prof. Josef Schmid zum 70. Geburtstag* (ed. J. Blinzler, O. Kuss, and F. Mussner; Regensburg: Pustet, 1963), 125–37 (repr. in Kilpatrick's *Principles and Practice of New Testament Textual Criticism: Collected Essays of G. D. Kilpatrick* [ed. J. K. Elliott; Bibliotheca ephemeridum theologicarum lovaniensium 96; Leuven: Leuven University Press/Peeters, 1990], 15–32). See also J. K. Elliott, "The United Bible Societies Greek New Testament: An Evaluation," *Novum Testamentum* 15 (1973): 298–99; idem, "The Atticist Grammarians" [Phrynichus and Moeris], in Elliott's *Essays and Studies in New Testament Textual Criticism* (Estudios de Filología Neotestamentaria 3; Cordova: El Almendro, 1992), 65–77; this chapter is adapted from two earlier works, yet they do not take into account the critiques of Colwell, Martini, or Fee referred to in the following discussion and notes (but see n. 28 below). M. W. Holmes ("Reasoned Eclecticism in New Testament Textual Criticism," in *TNTCR* 339 n. 11) points out that Günther Zuntz already in 1946 included Atticist tendencies among his criteria.
19. E. C. Colwell, "Hort Redivivus: A Plea and a Program," in *Transitions in Biblical Scholarship* (ed. J. C. Rylaarsdam; Essays in Divinity 6; Chicago: University of Chicago Press, 1968), 137–38 (repr. in Colwell's *Studies in Methodology in Textual Criticism of the New Testament* [New Testament Tools and Studies 9; Leiden: Brill, 1969], 154–55).
20. C. M. Martini, "Eclecticism and Atticism in the Textual Criticism of the Greek New Testament," in *On Language, Culture, and Religion: In Honor of Eugene A. Nida* (ed. M. Black and W. A. Smalley; The Hague: Mouton, 1974), 151–55.
21. G. D. Fee, "Rigorous or Reasoned Eclecticism—Which?" in *Studies in New Testament Language and Text: Essays in Honour of George D. Kilpatrick on the Occasion of His Sixty-Fifth Birthday* (ed. J. K. Elliott; Novum Testamentum Supplement 44; Leiden: Brill, 1976), 184–91 (= *STM* 131–36).

liott defended the Atticizing principle against its detractors,[22] but some textual critics currently are reluctant to employ it.

But it is the shorter-reading argument that has received the most vigorous reassessment in the past three decades or so. This argument says that the shorter/shortest reading in a variation unit has priority because—as most of us have repeated time and again—scribes tend to expand the text rather than to shorten it (to quote one of my own statements). It was Ernest Colwell, in 1965, who provided the impetus for a critique of this principle in his analysis of variants in the singular readings (i.e., unique readings—found nowhere else) of three early, extensive New Testament papyri, $\mathfrak{P}^{45}$, $\mathfrak{P}^{66}$, and $\mathfrak{P}^{75}$; his aim was to discern individual scribal habits. His result regarding omissions and additions—that each scribe more frequently omitted than added material[23]—caught the interest of James Royse, whose investigation doubled the number of early manuscripts by using $\mathfrak{P}^{45}$, $\mathfrak{P}^{46}$, $\mathfrak{P}^{47}$, $\mathfrak{P}^{66}$, $\mathfrak{P}^{72}$, and $\mathfrak{P}^{75}$; tightened the methodology in this meticulous exercise; and reached the same result: "The general tendency during the early period of textual transmission was to omit," and, therefore, "other things being equal, one should prefer the longer reading."[24] Thoroughgoing eclectics, of whom Elliott is currently the foremost advocate and practitioner, follow this reversal of the shorter-reading principle. Elliott, in one of

22. G. D. Kilpatrick, "Eclecticism and Atticism," *Ephemerides theologicae lovanienses* 53 (1977): 107–12 (repr. in Kilpatrick's *Principles and Practice*, 73–79) (response to Martini); J. K. Elliott, "Thoroughgoing Eclecticism in New Testament Textual Criticism," in *TNTCR* 326–27 (response to Fee).

23. E. C. Colwell, "Scribal Habits in Early Papyri: A Study in the Corruption of the Text," in *The Bible in Modern Scholarship: Papers Read at the 100th Meeting of the Society of Biblical Literature, December 28–30, 1964* (ed. J. Philip Hyatt; Nashville: Abingdon, 1965), 370–89 (repr. as "Method in Evaluating Scribal Habits: A Study of $\mathfrak{P}^{45}$, $\mathfrak{P}^{66}$, $\mathfrak{P}^{75}$," in Colwell's *Studies in Methodology in Textual Criticism of the New Testament* [New Testament Tools and Studies 9; Leiden: Brill, 1969], 106–24). His analysis is discussed by K. Junack, "Abschreibpraktiken und Schreibergewohnheiten in ihrer Auswirkung auf die Textüberlieferung," in *New Testament Textual Criticism: Its Significance for Exegesis: Essays in Honour of Bruce M. Metzger* (ed. E. J. Epp and G. D. Fee; Oxford: Clarendon, 1981), 288–92.

24. J. R. Royse, "Scribal Tendencies in the Transmission of the Text of the New Testament," in *TNTCR* 239–52, esp. 242–47, quotation from 246. See also idem, "Scribal Habits in the Transmission of New Testament Texts," in *The Critical Study of Sacred Texts* (ed. Wendy Doniger O'Flaherty; Berkeley Religious Studies Series 2; Berkeley: Graduate Theological Union, 1979), 139–61;

his two most recent formulations of his eclectic method, argues that, "in general, the longer text is more likely to be original providing that that text is consistent with the language, style, and theology of the context" because "in general, manuscripts tended to be accidentally shortened rather than deliberately lengthened in the process of copying."[25]

As Royse readily acknowledges—and as others point out— the matter is not quite that simple, and, indeed, he offers some caveats of his own. For example, Royse rightly states that his evidence relates to and questions the validity of the shorter-reading criterion only for the "earliest period of the transmission of the New Testament text,"[26] leading him to a further conclusion that "as a rule early scribes did not exercise the care evidenced in later transcriptions."[27] Royse also recognizes that "normal" scribal behavior (such as his detailed analysis uncovers) does not explain, for example, the 7%–8% greater length of the D-text of Acts over against the B-text,[28] nor, one might add, does it ex-

---

idem, "The Treatment of Scribal Leaps in Metzger's *Textual Commentary*," *New Testament Studies* 29 (1983): 539–51. The impracticality of the criterion is argued by E. Tov, *The Text-Critical Use of the Septuagint in Biblical Research* (2d ed.; Jerusalem: Simor, 1997), 228–30; idem, "Criteria for Evaluating Textual Readings: The Limitation of Textual Rules," *Harvard Theological Review* 75 (1982): 440–41; idem, *Textual Criticism of the Hebrew Bible*, 305–7. For a response to Royse and Tov, see M. Silva, "Internal Evidence in the Text-Critical Use of the LXX," in *La Septuaginta en la investigación contemporánea (V Congreso de la IOSCS)* (ed. N. Fernández Marcos; Madrid: Instituto Arias Montano, 1985), 154–64; idem, "The Text of Galatians: Evidence from the Earliest Greek Manuscripts," in *Scribes and Scripture: New Testament Essays in Honor of J. Harold Greenlee* (ed. D. A. Black; Winona Lake, Ind.: Eisenbrauns, 1992), 23–24 (who counts all omissions/additions, not just those in singular readings).

25. J. K. Elliott, "Can We Recover the Original Text of the New Testament? An Examination of the Rôle of Thoroughgoing Eclecticism," in Elliott's *Essays and Studies in New Testament Textual Criticism* (Estudios de Filología Neotestamentaria 3; Cordova: El Almendro, 1992), 40; see also idem, "Thoroughgoing Eclecticism," 327.

26. Royse, "Scribal Habits," 155.

27. Royse, "Scribal Tendencies," 248.

28. Royse, "Scribal Habits," 156. On the differing length of the B-text and D-text of Acts, see the recent study of J. Read-Heimerdinger, "The 'Long' and 'Short' Texts of Acts: A Closer Look at the Quantity and Types of Variation," *Revista catalana de teología* 22 (1997): 245–61. She concludes (247) that the D-text is 6.6% longer than the B-text.

plain items such as the additional endings of Mark or the Pericope Adulterae, or numerous smaller phrases (unless homoeoteleuton and homoeoarcton—scribal leaps from the same to the same—can be identified confidently). One reason for this is that Royse's methodology of analyzing scribal habits only from the singular readings of a manuscript yields omissions that, perhaps more than half the time, consist of a single word.[29] Yet, he has certainly chosen the best research model if one wants to ascertain in the most accurate fashion a particular scribe's own foibles, for his procedure avoids the inclusion in the study of previous scribal errors—those already present in the manuscript the scribe is copying—and thereby assures the least contaminated data. Moisés Silva points this out but also reminds Royse and us that a fuller profile of a particular scribe's habits and of the manuscript being produced requires that all variants need to be taken into account and that we need to know what kinds of omissions are involved (whether very brief omissions, including single words, homoeoteleuton, intentional alterations, etc.) and how many affect the sense of the passage.[30] In other words, judgments must be made as to whether omissions were accidental or intentional, followed by a count of each type. So, when Royse's full and fully updated study appears in the near future,[31] we will have a rich database on early scribal habits based on singular readings, but also one from which further studies can be launched.

This assessment is meant to imply that we should not give up entirely on the shorter-reading criterion, though it may well turn out that Michael Holmes is correct when he states that "in the light of Royse's study the venerable canon of *lectio brevior potior* is now seen as relatively useless, at least for the early papyri."[32]

29. Silva, "Internal Evidence," 159 n. 24.
30. Silva, "Text of Galatians," 23; idem, "Internal Evidence," 158; see 157–61. See Hurtado, "Beyond the Interlude?" 37, for a similar qualification: "Head and Royse agree in showing that omission is much more common than addition, *at least in unintentional scribal tendencies*" (emphasis added).
31. To be published in the series Studies and Documents under the tentative title *Scribal Habits in Early Greek New Testament Manuscripts*.
32. Holmes, "Reasoned Eclecticism," 343.

It may still be worthwhile, however, to ponder the usefulness of the shorter-reading criterion in view of some relatively recent studies that appear to support one side of the issue or the other. For example, Silva offers a ministudy of Galatians variants in $\mathfrak{P}^{46}$ and the three major Pauline parchment manuscripts of the fourth and fifth centuries: Sinaiticus, Vaticanus, and Alexandrinus. In the process, he sorts the variants into categories, such as (mere) function words, phrases, and so on, and watches for omissions likely due to homoeoteleuton; his results show, for example, five additions in $\mathfrak{P}^{46}$ against thirty-three omissions, though most of these variants are function words or explicable by homoeoteleuton.[33] Peter Head studies the singular readings of fourteen fragmentary New Testament papyri and finds twelve different omissions against seven additions. He admits that the sample is small, precluding firm conclusions, though he claims that his results "fully support" Royse's finding that "omission is more common than addition."[34] Finally, Jenny Read-Heimerdinger presents a quantitative analysis of types of variation between Codex Vaticanus (B) and Codex Bezae (D), including additions and omissions. While not prejudging the relationship between the two manuscripts (i.e., referring to an "omission" in D is not meant to imply that B was original and D was secondary), the statistical result shows that (over against B) Codex D "adds" 1,448 words while it "omits" 579 words.[35] Though this is a very different kind of study from those considered above, it may nonetheless be relevant to the shorter-reading discussion and one that invites discrimination among unintentional and intentional alterations.

Two other criteria or arguments were challenged in recent decades, including the well-established "author's style" argument,

33. Silva, "Text of Galatians," 23–24.
34. P. M. Head, "Observations on Early Papyri of the Synoptic Gospels, Especially on the 'Scribal Habits,'" *Biblica* 71 (1990): 240–47, esp. 246–47.
35. Read-Heimerdinger, "'Long' and 'Short' Texts of Acts," 245–61, esp. 250–51. The issue is complex, of course, because, if one were to assume that the D-text (or, more precisely, the primitive text behind it) was earlier than B, the result would be that B omits 1,448 words, while adding only 579 over against D. Cf. also M. Black, "Notes on the Longer and the Shorter Text of Acts," in *On Language, Culture, and Religion: In Honor of Eugene A. Nida* (ed. M. Black and W. A. Smalley; Approaches to Semiotics 56; The Hague: Mouton, 1974), 119–31.

namely, that the reading has priority that best conforms to the author's style. The basis for objection was that "it cannot be expected or presupposed that the language employed in the New Testament documents will of necessity be consistent."[36] This should be tested further; yet, employed in a contextual manner along with other arguments, it appears to function about as well as many—all of which require appropriate qualification. Second, the very old argument that the harder reading is preferable is characterized as too subjective to be practical by Emanuel Tov, among the leading textual critics of the Hebrew Bible and the Septuagint. Once, however, obvious scribal errors are ignored and other reasonable qualifications are employed, as Silva, again, points out, the principle functions well enough; after all, these internal arguments are not "rules" that operate automatically, but require adaptation to the various specific contexts of textual variation.[37]

Finally, as we have intimated all along, it is important to understand how these arguments for priority of readings function—both the external and the internal—and, above all, to recognize that they do not operate in a mechanical fashion as if they were tests to be applied *seriatim* to a variation unit, which—if a variant passes all of them—accredit that reading. On the contrary, many will not be relevant to a given variation unit or, what is more troublesome, in a single case one or more criteria may accredit one reading, while other arguments support a competing reading. For example, in Matthew 6:33 a read-

---

36. J. H. Petzer, "Author's Style and the Textual Criticism of the New Testament," *Neotestamentica* 24 (1990): 185–97, esp. 192–96, quotation from 186. See Petzer's later "Eclecticism and the Text of the New Testament," in *Text and Interpretation: New Approaches in the Criticism of the New Testament* (ed. P. J. Hartin and J. H. Petzer; New Testament Tools and Studies 15; Leiden: Brill, 1991), 58–59.

37. Tov, *Text-Critical Use of the Septuagint*, 228–30; idem, "Criteria for Evaluating Textual Readings," 439–40; idem, with more examples, *Textual Criticism of the Hebrew Bible*, 302–5; B. Albrektson, "Difficilior Lectio Probabilior— A Rule of Textual Criticism and Its Use in Old Testament Studies," *Oudtestamentische Studiën* 21 (1981): 5–18. For the response to Tov and a positive evaluation of the criterion in New Testament use, see Silva, "Internal Evidence," 154–57. Further in defense of the criterion, see E. A. Nida, "The 'Harder Reading' in Textual Criticism: An Application of the Second Law of Thermodynamics," *Bible Translator* 32 (1981): 101–7.

ing that explains the others competes with a reading that better conforms to Matthew's style. At other times, a variant may be the harder reading, while a competing variant may be strongly supported by old and geographically diverse manuscripts.[38] At this point the felicitous phrase *balance of probabilities* comes into play: a process by which we measure each variant against both the external and the internal arguments for relevance, compare the results by weighing any competing arguments against one another, and form a reasonable judgment—that is, choose the most probable reading. This, I hasten to add, is not for the reason suggested in these lines from "The Painter Who Pleased Nobody" by John Gay in the early eighteenth century:

> Lest men suspect your tale untrue,
> Keep probability in view.

Moreover, in the course of measuring two or more readings in a variation unit, we soon discover that even the more clearly empirical data we have (as found in the external canons) must be applied with art and skill, just as required for the internal arguments. Yet, even if the various arguments conflict with one another, that does not mean that they should be discarded; it only means that they are more sophisticated than simple "rules." Taking another example, if the history of the text is incomplete, that does not mean that it cannot be written or that what has been constructed has no merit; it means only that we must work harder to interpret and integrate the data we have.

Though this issue is far more complex than this brief treatment suggests, as the end of the nineteenth century approached, New Testament textual criticism had arrived at two sets of guidelines or arguments for measuring the priority of variant readings: external and internal. Now, a century later, we have the same two sets, with one or two items added and one or two deleted from the internal side. We also find, unlike a century ago, that thoroughgoing or rigorous eclectics, such as Kilpatrick

38. The use of internal evidence is illustrated profusely in the works of G. D. Kilpatrick (see his *Principles and Practice of New Testament Textual Criticism*) and J. K. Elliott (see his *Essays and Studies in New Testament Textual Criticism*). A perusal of Metzger's *TCGNT* quickly illumines the balance and also the alternation of external and internal arguments.

and Elliott, give relatively less weight to the external list and rely rather on the internal considerations—a subject beyond this presentation.

In what precedes, however, I have almost totally neglected the external arguments, where my own major interest lies and my work has been concentrated. In the 1980s I spoke of the "crisis of criteria," expressing the hope that both the external and internal considerations could be made more effective, but expecting that more progress could be made on the external side— the historical-documentary approach that would enable us to write the history of the New Testament text and thereby largely obviate or at least significantly reduce the need for the internal arguments.[39] After all, Westcott and Hort had written, to their satisfaction, a rather clear history of the text that isolated for them the "best" documentary witnesses, and why couldn't we do much better since they had virtually no early papyri to aid them. Of course, I knew very well that they had employed internal arguments to accredit their so-called best manuscripts,[40] but we had the Chester Beatty and Bodmer papyri and more to assist in our reconstruction of the history of transmission. Indeed, we now have 116 New Testament papyri, representing perhaps 112 different manuscripts, of which 61, or 54%, date prior to around the turn of the third/fourth centuries. Should we not be able to write the very early history of our text—something that the vast majority of textual critics are convinced would improve our external arguments?

Have we made progress on the internal side? Wherever discussion and debate have raised questions, generated hypotheses, devised tests and evaluative methods, and even weakened the efficacy of existing principles, progress is evident, but it is far from adequate. And if present means for testing and refinement are lacking or insufficient, we need to develop new procedures, better methods. Michael Holmes, at the conclusion of a similar discussion, affirmed that "the primary effect of recent discussions of the various [internal] criteria . . . has been to in-

39. E. J. Epp, "Textual Criticism," in *The New Testament and Its Modern Interpreters* (ed. E. J. Epp and G. W. MacRae; Philadelphia: Fortress/Atlanta: Scholars Press, 1989), 100–103 (= *STM* 39–42).
40. Extended discussion may be found in my "Eclectic Method," 236–42 (= *STM* 158–63).

crease our skepticism. We are less sure than ever that their use
. . . will produce any certainty with regard to the results obtained."[41] I do not disagree, because skepticism can be a pro-
ductive reaction, instigating renewed investigation and fresh insights. I would not, therefore, interpret recent work as lacking
in progress or the future as devoid of hope. In the twenty-first
century we can and will refine *both* the external and internal arguments.

Choosing among Manuscripts—and Deciding on Groups: The Issue of Text-Types

The relative emphasis placed upon external and internal considerations in the evaluation of variants divides textual critics
into two classes (though theoretically into three).[42] On the one
hand are thoroughgoing or rigorous eclectics, who utilize internal arguments largely to the exclusion of the external. (Theoretically, there should be an opposite class, historical-documentary
eclectics, or the like, who emphasize external considerations to
the virtual exclusion of the internal, but I know of no one currently who fits into such a group.) So, in reality, on the other hand
are reasoned eclectics, as they are named, who employ a combi-
nation of external and internal arguments, applied evenly and
without prejudice (though, admittedly, many lean toward the external whenever appropriate or even as often as they dare), with
the goal of reaching a reasonable decision based on the relative
probabilities among all applicable arguments for priority.

When we now turn to the issue of New Testament text-
types—that is, the attempt to isolate clusters of manuscripts
that constitute distinguishable kinds of texts as evidenced by
similar textual characteristics, with the further goal of utilizing

41. Holmes, "Reasoned Eclecticism," 343. J. H. Petzer draws a more extreme conclusion: "There is still no more certainty with regard to our choices
of readings than a century ago"; see "A Survey of the Developments in the Textual Criticism of the Greek New Testament since UBS³," *Neotestamentica* 24
(1990): 82.
42. For detailed descriptions, see Epp, "Eclectic Method," 244–57 (= *STM*
164–73); idem, "Textual Criticism in the Exegesis of the New Testament," 61–
64, 70–73.

them to sketch the history of the New Testament text—it will be obvious that reasoned eclectics take a great interest in the enterprise while thoroughgoing or rigorous eclectics tend not to do so. This is because text-types are established largely (though not exclusively) on the basis of external evidence—and they themselves then become an element of external evidence as part of the argument that priority may be granted to a variant supported by "one or more established groups of manuscripts of recognized antiquity, character, and perhaps location."[43] After all, text-types can be characterized as to age and quality—though internal evidence is employed in judging the latter.

The establishment of text-types (though I prefer the term *textual clusters*)[44] is an integral part of the textual critic's attempt to reconstruct the history of the New Testament text by tracing the lines of transmission back through the extant manuscripts to the earliest stages and then selecting the readings that seem best to represent the earliest attainable level of the textual tradition. In theory, at least, we should be able to organize our extant manuscripts into groups or clusters, each of which has a similar kind or character of text. Next, as a result of this process, we should be able to isolate the earliest known group or groups. Then we should be able to identify other groups that can be arranged in chronological succession—that is, later groups. If only one very early group or cluster were to emerge, that would simplify matters a great deal, for it could be claimed with a high measure of legitimacy that this earliest type of text is closest to the text (or a text) of the early Christian community. Or, to view the matter at the level of readings, within each variation unit the reading would be selected that comes from that earliest cluster (other things being equal, as we say—i.e., after also applying the internal arguments), again with a plausible claim that it represents the or a text of the early or earliest period.

43. External criterion 4 in my list in "Eclectic Method," 243 (=*STM* 163); idem, "Texual Criticism in the Exegesis of the New Testament," 72.
44. See my "Significance of the Papyri for Determining the Nature of the New Testament Text in the Second Century: A Dynamic View of Textual Transmission," in *Gospel Traditions in the Second Century: Origins, Recensions, Text, and Transmission* (ed. W. L. Petersen; Christianity and Judaism in Antiquity 3; Notre Dame: University of Notre Dame Press, 1989), 84–101 (= *STM* 283–95); idem, "Textual Criticism (NT)," 430–31.

This—though much oversimplified—is the traditional method of historical-documentary textual criticism (as I call it),[45] so named because it places the greater emphasis on external criteria, including the age of documents, their provenance (if known), their place in the history of the text, and the general quality of their scribes and their texts as a whole.

As it turns out, however, this process of grouping (according to most scholars) isolates not one earliest New Testament group or text-type, but two early clusters: the B-text and the D-text, though the latter is a matter of some debate. How is the general age or antiquity of a text-type established? Primarily by the age of the oldest manuscripts that are found in the resulting groups; to be more exact, however, it is not the age of a manuscript that counts but the age of the text it contains, thereby complicating the matter considerably. A second and significant factor in determining the antiquity of a text-type is to identify any early church writers who support readings characteristic of each group. Indeed, the latter is of great importance because coincidence of readings between a given manuscript and church writings provides a reasonably objective verification of the age of the readings in question—dependent, of course, on the degree to which our critical editions of patristic sources are reliable.

Naturally, if we have two early text-types, followed by one or more later text-types, a rather simplistic kind of historical-documentary approach will not work. It is at this point that those otherwise naturally inclined toward a historical-documentary approach will embrace reasoned eclecticism and will utilize with vigor both the external and internal arguments for the priority of readings.

New Testament textual critics began to place manuscripts into classes or groups at least as far back as Bengel (1740), whose Asiatic (i.e., later) and African (ancient) families were expanded by J. S. Semler in 1767 to three groups comparable to our own three main text-types: Alexandrian (≈ B-text), Western (≈ D-text), and Oriental (≈ A-text or Byzantine).[46] By the end of the nineteenth century a clear-cut proposal by WH was widely accepted: two

---

45. For discussion, see Epp, "Textual Criticism," 92–94 (= *STM* 32–34); idem, "Textual Criticism (NT)," 432.
46. M. R. Vincent, *A History of the Textual Criticism of the New Testament* (New York: Macmillan, 1903), 89–93.

early text-types, inappropriately named "Neutral" for the B-text and "Western" for the D-text, and one later Syrian text-type, commonly designated the *textus receptus*. Equally broadly accepted, at least for the moment, was WH's conclusion that the original text is generally to be identified with the Neutral or B-text. This made the Western or D-text an equally early but corrupt text parallel to the Neutral text, with the Syrian or Byzantine text-type a later, conflated version built largely upon the other two. This nuanced form of Hort's view soon faced criticism and redevelopment, but this is where the issue of text-types stood as the nineteenth century moved toward its conclusion.

Before the century ended, however, the discovery of early New Testament papyri at Oxyrhynchus, beginning in 1898, cast bright rays of sunshine down through the entire twentieth century and became the harbinger of many more discoveries of early and extensive New Testament papyri—culminating (for the moment, at least) in a third-/fourth-century Oxyrhynchus papyrus containing some three hundred lines from twelve chapters of the Apocalypse of John ($\mathfrak{P}^{115}$), published in 1999—in which, incidentally, the "number of the Beast" is 616 (as in Codex C) instead of 666 (Revelation 13:18). Such manuscripts, but more so the Chester Beatty ($\mathfrak{P}^{45}$, $\mathfrak{P}^{46}$, $\mathfrak{P}^{47}$) and Bodmer papyri ($\mathfrak{P}^{66}$, $\mathfrak{P}^{72}$, $\mathfrak{P}^{75}$), published in the 1930s and 1950s respectively, provided rich and fresh material for the construction of text-types, though by no means was it always clear just where the contribution of these new papyri lay, especially with the highly fragmentary ones.

Modifications to the WH scheme of text-types appeared as the twentieth century proceeded, though not at first because of the papyri. A major development was the identification of a Caesarean text of the Gospels, first by Kirsopp Lake and Robert Blake, then elaborated by B. H. Streeter and further by Lake, Blake, and Silva New, as well as others.[47] In addition, the D-text became a matter of discussion and debate, involving questions such as whether it was closer to the original than the B-text; whether it was rough and

---

47. K. Lake and R. P. Blake, "The Text of the Gospels and the Koridethi Codex," *Harvard Theological Review* 16 (1923): 267–86; B. H. Streeter, *The Four Gospels: A Study of Origins, Treating of the Manuscript Tradition, Sources, Authorship, and Dates* (London: Macmillan, 1924), 77–108; K. Lake, R. P. Blake, and S. New, "The Caesarean Text of the Gospel of Mark," *Harvard Theological Review* 21 (1928): 207–404.

early, or corrupt and later; whether the author of Luke–Acts wrote one edition or two; whether the D-text represents an early text-type or only a later one; and so on—issues, by the way, that remain largely unresolved or at least debated even today.[48]

Where do we stand at the outset of the twenty-first century? The scheme I advocate identifies (1) an early cluster desig-nated the B-text, with roots in the second century and repre-sented chiefly by $\mathfrak{P}^{75}$ and Codex B; (2) a perhaps equally early D-text (represented chiefly by some fragmentary papyri, Codex D, the Old Latin, and the Old Syriac [in part]); (3) an abortive C-text (in Mark, represented by $\mathfrak{P}^{45}$ and Codex W but continu-ing no farther);[49] and (4) a later cluster, the A-text (represented by Codex A and most later majuscules and minuscules).[50] Kurt Aland and Barbara Aland, however, do not assign to the D-text a date earlier than the fourth century, nor to any others; for them, "not until the fourth century . . . did the formation of text types begin."[51] They do, however, speak of Codex D's "very few precursors" and list in their category IV (= D-text) two third-century papyri ($\mathfrak{P}^{48}$, $\mathfrak{P}^{69}$) and two third-/fourth-century

48. Recent arguments for and against the priority of the D-text are summa-rized in J. H. Petzer, "The History of the New Testament Text—Its Reconstruc-tion, Significance and Use in New Testament Textual Criticism," in *New Testament Textual Criticism, Exegesis, and Early Church History: A Discussion of Methods* (ed. B. Aland and J. Delobel; Contributions to Biblical Exegesis and Theology 7; Kampen, Netherlands: Kok Pharos, 1994), 18–25.

49. Note that the Caesarean text is no longer listed in Metzger's *TCGNT*: it appears on pp. xxix–xxx of the first edition, but its representatives are nowhere to be found on p. 15* of the second edition, though their text is described (6*) as "a mixture of Western [D-text] and Alexandrian [B-text] readings." Indeed, I had earlier designated this the C-text because in textual character (just as Metzger says) it stands midway between the B-text and D-text; see Epp, "Twen-tieth-Century Interlude," 393–96 (= *STM* 89–92); idem, "Significance of the Pa-pyri," 88 (= *STM* 285); idem, "Textual Criticism (NT)," 431. The major work resulting in the demise of the Caesarean text is L. W. Hurtado, *Text-Critical Methodology and the Pre-Caesarean Text: Codex W in the Gospel of Mark* (Stud-ies and Documents 43; Grand Rapids: Eerdmans, 1981); see the conclusions, 85–89. Though family 13 is often associated with this text, Hurtado argues that it is a secondary and not a primary witness.

50. For discussion of this structure, see Epp, "Twentieth-Century Inter-lude," 392–400 (= *STM* 88–95); idem, "Significance of the Papyri," 84–88 (= *STM* 283–86); idem, "Textual Criticism," 97–100 (= *STM* 37–39); idem, "Tex-tual Criticism (NT)," 430–31.

51. Aland and Aland, *Text of the New Testament*, 64.

manuscripts ($\mathfrak{P}^{38}$, 0171) prior to the fifth-century (or possibly late fourth-century) Codex D.[52] The difference is that many textual critics, contrary to the Alands, consider that to be evidence of a textual cluster—existing at least by the third century. As noted, however, the Alands are willing to identify three text-types, but only from 300 C.E. and after: "the Alexandrian text, the Koine text, and the D text"—that is, our B-text, A-text (or Byzantine), and D-text, respectively, but not a Caesarean text.[53]

There is also difference of opinion among textual critics as to which fragmentary papyri can be placed in these groups with confidence, due to the small number of variant readings in many of them. What is clear and significant, however, is that no pre-sixth-century papyri support the A-text.[54]

The status of the text-type issue at the outset of the twenty-first century, then, is that virtually all textual critics accept the existence, at least by 300 C.E., of three text-types (B, D, and A). Though many believe that a C-text (but no longer to be called Caesarean) existed in the early fourth century, it is not essential to the basic documentary history of the New Testament text generally postulated—that is, the three text-types around 300. As for the crucial period preceding the fourth century, two views are dominant. The first view is that of Kurt Aland and Barbara Aland, who evaluate and categorize the witnesses in this early period according to their manner of transmission (rather than by similarity of readings), and they suggest four degrees of fidelity in the copying of exemplars:

1. Some manuscripts were transmitted with *normal* care (i.e., relatively faithfully, with a limited amount of varia-

52. Ibid., 65, 159; see 64 (which speaks of some forms of the text before 300 that "anticipated or were more closely akin to the D text") and 93 (where $\mathfrak{P}^{38}$, $\mathfrak{P}^{48}$, and $\mathfrak{P}^{69}$ "may be regarded as precursors or branches of the D text"). At the April 2000 symposium at Southeastern Seminary, J. K. Elliott alerted me to an Oxyrhynchus papyrus of Acts, not yet numbered or published, that appears to be of the D-text-type (I am unaware of the date assigned to the manuscript).
53. Ibid., 66–67.
54. Papyri that represent or were influenced by the Byzantine text are $\mathfrak{P}^{63}$ (ca. 500), $\mathfrak{P}^{84}$ (sixth century), $\mathfrak{P}^{68}$, perhaps $\mathfrak{P}^{73}$ and $\mathfrak{P}^{74}$ (seventh century), and $\mathfrak{P}^{42}$ (seventh/eighth century).

tion and keeping "significantly closer to the pattern of the original text").

2. Some manuscripts were copied from their exemplars with *strict* (i.e., meticulous) care.

3. Some manuscripts were passed along in a relatively *free* manner (i.e., with greater variation than normal).

4. Some manuscripts were transmitted in a *paraphrastic* fashion (i.e., in the manner of the D-text), with the last two categories showing the "most diverse variants."[55]

Then the Alands employ two overlapping groups of manuscripts to reconstruct the "text of the early period," which for all practical purposes means, for them, the original text.[56] While they rely on manuscripts transmitted in a strict manner, they depend more heavily on those passed along in a normal fashion, combined with all papyri and majuscules that date prior to or around the turn of the third/fourth centuries, for these witnesses (now totaling sixty-one) have "inherent significance" by virtue of predating the text-type era.[57] In addition, they state that the text circulated in this period in the four specified Textforms (not text-types) without any ecclesiastical control.[58]

55. Aland and Aland, *Text of the New Testament*, 64, 93, 95. The classification system is more complex than the above summary, for there are in-between or qualified classifications as well, such as "at least normal" ($\mathfrak{P}^{15}$, $\mathfrak{P}^{22}$, $\mathfrak{P}^{30}$, $\mathfrak{P}^{32}$, $\mathfrak{P}^{49}$, $\mathfrak{P}^{53}$, $\mathfrak{P}^{77}$), "strict text, somewhat carelessly written" ($\mathfrak{P}^{70}$), "very free text" ($\mathfrak{P}^{69}$), and "free text, carelessly written" ($\mathfrak{P}^{40}$) Also, not all manuscripts are assigned a classification.

56. K. Aland, "The Twentieth-Century Interlude in New Testament Textual Criticism," in *Text and Interpretation: Studies in the New Testament Presented to Matthew Black* (ed. E. Best and R. McL. Wilson; Cambridge: Cambridge University Press, 1979), 11; idem, "Der neue 'Standard-Text' in seinem Verhältnis zu den frühen Papyri und Majuskeln," in *New Testament Textual Criticism: Its Significance for Exegesis: Essays in Honour of Bruce M. Metzger* (ed. E. J. Epp and G. D. Fee; Oxford: Clarendon, 1981), 274–75 (note that the term *standard text* has been replaced by *new text* in subsequent publications); Aland and Aland, *Text of the New Testament*, 333; cf. 335.

57. Aland and Aland, *Text of the New Testament*, 93, 95; see the list of forty-seven pre-third-/fourth-century manuscripts on 56–57. With the publication of $\mathfrak{P}^{98}$ and of thirteen early Oxyrhynchus papyri, the total is now sixty-one early New Testament manuscripts.

58. Ibid., 59, 64; see the categories assigned to papyri through $\mathfrak{P}^{96}$ on 96–102. For a careful description of this "Münster theory," see Petzer, "History of the New Testament Text," 30–35.

I have no strong objection to this general view that in the early period the New Testament text was transmitted in varying Textforms and without controls, except that the Alands' fourfold categorization seems patently to be based on a circular argument, for the witnesses claimed to preserve most faithfully the original text are at the same time the manuscripts employed to construct the NA and UBS editions, which, in turn, are claimed to be the virtual original text. If, for the sake of argument, an editor thought that the precursors of the Alands' D-text best represented the original text (on the grounds, e.g., that it is rough and therefore primitive), would not these precursors of D ($\mathfrak{P}^{38}$, $\mathfrak{P}^{48}$, $\mathfrak{P}^{69}$, and 0171) then likely be labeled normal and/or strict Textforms, with the presently designated strict and normal manuscripts called something else?[59]

The second view of the text in the pre-300 period is held, it is fair to say, by most textual critics[60]—and it is my own position as well. It argues that two early textual clusters or text-types (B and D) were functioning from perhaps as early as the second century, with a third text-type (A or Byzantine) developing later. Even in the early, uncontrolled period, many papyri share enough similarities in readings to be identified as clusters in conjunction with later manuscripts, although—as noted earlier—the fragmentary papyri often are difficult to place. Doing the best we can, however, we draw lines of connectedness between the earliest witnesses and

59. Epp, "New Testament Textual Criticism Past, Present, and Future: Reflections on the Alands' *Text of the New Testament,*" *Harvard Theological Review* 82 (1989): 223–26. See also B. D. Ehrman, "A Problem of Textual Circularity: The Alands on the Classification of New Testament Manuscripts," *Biblica* 70 (1989): 381 n. 19. Like my discussion, Ehrman's essay is devoted not primarily to the four categories discussed above but to the Alands' classification of manuscripts under five headings (I–V) that indicate the degree of relevance for establishing the original text; Ehrman, however, finds the same circularity there. Cf. Petzer, "History of the New Testament Text," who, in his description of the Alands' general approach, is not explicit about a circular argument, but points out that, for them, the Alexandrian text is "the vehicle by means of which the original text was most faithfully transmitted" (32) and is "*de facto* equal to the original text" and that "the Alexandrian text in N[26] is explicitly acknowledged and used as a point of departure and decisive norm for the study of variant readings" (34).

60. Petzer, "History of the New Testament Text," 15: "Beyond dispute today seems to be the fact of the existence of these three main text-types."

any later manuscripts that share similar textual characteristics, and we conclude that the resulting clusters form the various text-types. The resulting schema—given the proper cautions—permits both the larger clusters and individual readings to be placed in a temporal continuum, with a good probability of tracing the textual footprints back to the earliest possible levels. This is not the place to review various attempts to match manuscripts with others of similar textual complexion,[61] but it is of current interest to note that the rather extensive third-/fourth-century $\mathfrak{P}^{115}$, published only in 1999, enters the picture as "the earliest witness" to the A/C-type of text of the Apocalypse of John, a text that, says David Parker, now—in the light of $\mathfrak{P}^{115}$—may be "more carefully reconstructed."[62] In this connection, it is worth noting also that, while excluding text-types before approximately 300, nonetheless the Alands, for all practical purposes, trace out for us the lines not only of the pre-300 D-text, but also of the pre-300 B-text by their categorization of the earliest papyri (even though they do not group manuscripts by textual consanguinity but by degrees of faithfulness to their exemplars).[63]

61. See Epp, "Significance of the Papyri," 84–101 (= *STM* 283–95).

62. D. C. Parker, "The Newly Published Oxyrhynchus Papyrus of Revelation," a paper read at the 1999 Annual Meeting of the Society of Biblical Literature in Boston; see the abstract in *AAR-SBL Abstracts 1999* (Atlanta: AAR & SBL, 1999), 266. (Note that text-types for the Apocalypse of John are different from those in the rest of the New Testament.)

63. To arrive at this conclusion, I compared my lists of papyri up to and around the turn of the third/fourth centuries that appear to fit into the various text-types, namely, A, B, C, and D ("Significance of the Papyri," 100 [= *STM* 294]) and the Alands' list of category I papyri of the same period (Aland and Aland, *Text of the New Testament*, 159). Of their thirty-seven papyri in category I, twenty-five were somewhere in my lists, but fully twenty of those twenty-five were in my roster of B-text representatives. Since, according to the Alands, category I consists of "manuscripts with a very high proportion of the early text . . . , presumably the original text" (335) and since "most of the manuscripts of this category belong to the 'Alexandrian' text type [= B-text]" (335 n. 13), I interpret this striking overlap of the papyri in my B-text list with those in the Alands' category I as significant evidence that a pre-third-/fourth-century text-type can be traced through their category I and connected with the mid-fourth-century Codex B and other witnesses to that text-type. I take this position in spite of Petzer, "History of the New Testament Text," 36, who, in describing the Münster theory, asserts that "although one is tempted to associate these 'text-types' [i.e., the Alands' 'strict,' 'normal,' 'free' texts] with the traditional text-types, they are in fact very different, because their constituent parts are not necessarily genealogically related."

On either approach, then, we will have sketched out a history of the New Testament text, though the Alands' approach, it seems to me, is less clear and less objectively based than the second procedure. What remains to be determined is whether this understanding of the history of the text is merely a rough sketch or one that already has numerous elements of refinement. Although that is unclear, the main point is that there is sufficient agreement to conclude that the vast majority of textual critics worldwide are convinced that the development of the New Testament text can be traced from very early times to the period of the great majuscules, with some textual scholars taking one path of explanation and others another for the earliest portion of that period. Our task now is to move toward a greater measure of refinement, either by clarifying the Alands' categories and/or by firming up the constituent membership of early textual clusters.

Jacobus Petzer's excellent assessment of the history of the New Testament text and its reconstruction—exactly what we have been discussing here—provides a compact summary of what New Testament textual criticism has accomplished, in broad strokes, in the last two centuries. The nineteenth century, he says, "managed to solve the textual riddles of the fourth century and settled the question of the Byzantine text"; the twentieth century solved the mysteries of the third century (though I am not as sure as he is that we have finished the task); and, he concludes, it remains now for the twenty-first century "to solve the two remaining riddles, that of (a) . . . the nature of the earliest transmission of the text, or the second century, and (b) the nature of the original text and its relation to the 'autographs,' or the first century."[64] I agree completely that our next task is to clarify textual transmission in the second century, though I am less confident that any simple solutions—or any solutions at all—will come quickly with respect to the first century. One small reason for renewed optimism about the second century is that, whereas $\mathfrak{P}^{52}$, containing John's Gospel, used to be the only second-century papyrus of the New Testament, now there are

---

64. Petzer, "History of the New Testament Text," 36. Hurtado, "Beyond the Interlude?" 38–43, also stresses the cruciality of the second century—with which I wholeheartedly agree.

two or three more: $\mathfrak{P}^{90}$ (John), $\mathfrak{P}^{104}$ (Matthew), and perhaps $\mathfrak{P}^{98}$, (the Apocalypse of John).[65] Further analysis of the use by second-century church writers of books that were in the process of becoming canon in that period will also assist us. So, let us press the second century for the answers we want and need.

Choosing among Critical Editions—and Deciding for Compromise: The Issue of Current Critical Editions of the Greek New Testament

Critical editions of the Greek New Testament—from the first one *printed* in 1514 as volume five of the Complutensian Polyglot and from the first one *published* in 1516 by Erasmus to those of the present day—all contain texts that never existed in any actual, exact manuscript form, for (as everyone knows) they have been reconstructed by incorporating individual readings from a vast array of Greek manuscripts, using in the process the arguments for priority discussed above, comparisons with supporting versions and church writers, and insights from recognized text-types. If one wished a critical edition closely resembling an actual manuscript over extended portions, Tischendorf's eighth edition (giving great weight to his greatest discovery, Codex Sinaiticus) or WH (with their close reliance on Codex Vaticanus) might be chosen. At the other extreme, the unfinished *Greek-English Diglot for the Use of Translators* by George D. Kilpatrick, in which he employed his form of eclecticism in selecting readings, would,

---

65. Three other papyri date around 200: $\mathfrak{P}^{46}$, $\mathfrak{P}^{64+67}$, and $\mathfrak{P}^{66}$; while two others (both containing portions of Matthew) stem from the late second/early third century: $\mathfrak{P}^{103}$ (P.Oxy. 64:4403) and $\mathfrak{P}^{77}$ (P.Oxy. 34:2683+64:4405). Y. K. Kim proposed a first-century date (ca. 80) for $\mathfrak{P}^{46}$ ("Palaeographical Dating of $\mathfrak{P}^{46}$ to the Later First Century," *Biblica* 69 [1988]: 248–57). D. B. Wallace (review of Kim's *Biblica* article in *Bibliotheca Sacra* [1989]: 451–52) suggests that this proposal will attract as much attention as J. O'Callaghan's identification of 7Q5 as Mark 6:52–53 (mid-first century!), but obviously it has not; Wallace himself says "wait and see." Hurtado, "Beyond the Interlude?" 40 n. 38, reminds us that the editors of $\mathfrak{P}^{75}$ (V. Martin and R. Kasser, *Papyrus Bodmer XIV–XV* [Geneva: Bibliotheca Bodmeriana, 1961], 1:13) posed a date between 175 and 200 as most probable, but the beginning of the third century is the current view.

I presume, resemble any actual manuscript even less than other current editions.[66] Yet, the artificiality of our critical editions is a nonissue, for a critical edition of any ancient writing is by nature a reconstruction. The only way it could be identical to a particular manuscript is if the editor rejected every variant in every other manuscript; moreover, even a writing extant in only one manuscript inevitably requires a critical edition, for emendations invariably are requisite to explain nonsense or otherwise difficult readings when no basis of comparison is available.

When we ask about critical editions of the New Testament in the second half of the nineteenth century, we must remember that Codex Vaticanus (B) came to prominence and that Codex Sinaiticus (א) was discovered in this period, along with many more manuscripts. Tischendorf utilized these and other celebrated fourth- and fifth-century codices to produce his various critical editions of the New Testament, culminating in the eighth major edition of 1869–72, with an extensive apparatus still useful today. But the most influential critical *text* (there was no apparatus) was that of Westcott and Hort in 1881, and both Tischendorf and WH, as noted earlier, gave the greatest authority to the most ancient manuscripts, carrying through the principles exemplified in Irenaeus and Jerome of old and emphasized from the time of Bentley (1720) through Bengel (1742), supported by Griesbach (1775), but triumphant in Lachmann (1831, 1850). So, as the twentieth century approached, the WH critical text—similar in nature to that of Tischendorf—stood as the

66. Elliott (*Essays and Studies in New Testament Textual Criticism*, 28) says that the diglot fascicles "represent to some extent the conclusions of Kilpatrick's text-critical method, though [they] do not give the results of a completely thoroughgoing eclecticism." Fascicles of the diglot appeared as follows, issued for private circulation by the British and Foreign Bible Society: *Mark* (1958), *Matthew* (1959), *John* (1960), *The General Letters* (1961), *Luke* (1962), *The Pastoral Letters and Hebrews* (1963), *Romans and 1 and 2 Corinthians* (1964). See Metzger, *Text of the New Testament*, 177–78, 257; Aland and Aland, *Text of the New Testament*, 25, 32. The Alands report that the cessation of Kilpatrick's project was due to the shift of the British Bible Society's support to the newly launched UBS project, an action, they claim, that "simply expressed a basic recognition that the text of the *GNT*, as far as it had been completed, was superior to that of the diglot edition" (32).

monument of nineteenth-century New Testament textual criticism.[67] Yet, before the nineteenth century was out, several major works of Dean John William Burgon appeared, some posthumously, that reverted to the pre-Lachmannian view of preference for the *textus receptus*.[68] To be sure, WH pushed their case too far in the audacious title of their edition, *The New Testament in the Original Greek*, but the textual edifice they constructed so carefully by a synergism of external and internal evidence on a modern foundation laid some 160 years earlier was not likely to fall, though it was to be modified in various ways during the twentieth century and to give way to the now almost universal NA and UBS text. Modifications to WH arose primarily from the issues reviewed in the first two sections of this essay.

First, text-types figured largely in WH's theory; and that they continue to play a role in establishing the text, at least for the vast majority of textual critics, is obvious enough from our earlier treatment, but also from the descriptions in manuals and handbooks and, pointedly, in *TCGNT*, where the components of the currently accepted text-types are listed.[69] The differing viewpoints about pre-fourth-century text-types discussed earlier suggest that there might be correspondingly different opinions about the time frame assigned to the re-

67. Although the older Nestle editions are championed in Aland and Aland's *Text of the New Testament*, 19–22, 26–30, and their text—with that of the NA editions—is called "the dominant text for eighty . . . years," the Nestle text of 1898 and following did not attract the vigorous debate that the WH edition did, for there was no grand theory that lay behind the Nestle edition. On the principles for establishing the early Nestle text, see the discussion below.

68. E.g., J. W. Burgon, *The Last Twelve Verses of the Gospel according to S. Mark* (Oxford: Parker, 1871); idem, *The Revision Revised* (London: Murray, 1883); idem, *The Causes of the Corruption of the Traditional Text of the Holy Gospels* (ed. E. Miller; London: Bell, 1896); idem, *The Traditional Text of the Holy Gospels Vindicated and Established* (ed. E. Miller; London: Bell, 1896).

69. I speak of the continuing role of text-types in establishing the text as something affirmed "pointedly" in *TCGNT* because the Alands, who served on the UBS editorial committee, do not accept pre-fourth-century text-types; yet, *TCGNT* lists the traditional text-types and their manuscript members, *including pre-fourth-century papyri*. Note that the Caesarean text is diminished on *TCGNT* 6*–7* and is absent from the "Lists of Witnesses according to Type of Text" on 15*.

constructed text of a critical edition such as UBS/NA. On the
one hand, most of us who are convinced that at least two text-
types existed in the second century would claim that such a
critical text quite probably takes us back to that early period,
though many of that persuasion might be reluctant to make
claims about having reached the original text. On the other
hand—surprisingly, I think—Kurt Aland, who does not ac-
knowledge any pre-fourth-century text-types, nonetheless
claims that the recent NA editions do represent the original
text.[70] At first blush, would we not have expected a less abso-
lutist view? The explanation, of course, lies in the Alands' use
of their classifications (free, normal, strict, and paraphrastic
texts) and their five categories of manuscripts, of which category I designates "manuscripts with a very high proportion of
the early text . . . , presumably the original text,"[71] though, as
noted earlier (see n. 59 above), a circular argument operates
here.

Second, the discussion, refinement, and alteration of the arguments for priority of readings led to reassessment of numerous points in WH, especially by testing their use of both external and internal evidence—though the two can never quite be
separated. On the one hand, testing the internal arguments
employed by WH took various avenues, resulting in the ques-
tioning of some, the addition of a couple, and the refinement
of others (as considered earlier), leading, about halfway between the time of WH and our own time, to thoroughgoing
eclecticism in distinction from reasoned eclecticism. On the
other hand, WH's reliance on Codex B, along with ℵ, was
tested (to use Elliott's emotionally charged but not incorrect
phrase) to see whether their "cult of the best manuscripts" was

70. On K. Aland's equation of the NA text with the original, see n. 56 above.
Cf. Petzer, "History of the New Testament Text," 32–34, who notes: "Recently
B. Aland has explicitly stated that the original text, i.e. the text reflected in the
manuscript tradition, is something quite different from the autographs."
Petzer refers to B. Aland's "Die Münsteraner Arbeit am Text des Neuen Testaments und ihr Beitrag für die frühe Überlieferung des 2. Jahrhunderts: Eine
methodologische Betrachtung," in *Gospel Traditions in the Second Century: Origins, Recensions, Text, and Transmission* (ed. W. L. Petersen; Christianity and
Judaism in Antiquity 3; Notre Dame: University of Notre Dame Press, 1989),
68–69.
71. Aland and Aland, *Text of the New Testament*, 335.

justified.[72] The resultant general conclusion was that a single or merely a few manuscripts should not—could not—be the basis for a critical edition. Nonetheless, and ironically, even those editors who embraced this latter principle still came up with a critical text of the New Testament that was similar in large measure to the WH edition, including the various editions by Eberhard Nestle and Erwin Nestle (beginning in 1898, with Erwin taking over from his father in 1927), the NA editions (beginning in 1960 with the twenty-second edition), the UBS text (beginning in 1966 with the first edition), and finally the unified text adopted in 1975 for UBS³ (1975) and NA²⁶ (1979) and their successors (UBS⁴ and NA²⁷, issued in 1993). That these various post-WH texts remain close in textual character to WH is demonstrated by the Alands themselves, who report that, while NA²⁵ shows, for example, 2,047 differences from von Soden, 1,996 from Vogels, 1,161 from Bover, and 770 from Merk, it contains only 558 differences from WH.[73] This "relatively close relationship between Nestle and Westcott-Hort"[74] may appear to be an almost inevitable result of the methods employed by Eberhard Nestle for his editions, namely, comparing the texts of Tischendorf and WH, consulting a third edition when the two disagreed, and then printing as his text the reading of two agreeing editions, with the reading of the third put into the apparatus. Beginning in 1901 Nestle used

72. See Elliott, "Rational Criticism and the Text of the New Testament," *Theology* 75 (1972): 339–40; idem, "Can We Recover the Original Text?" *Theology* 77 (1974): 345; idem, *Essays and Studies in New Testament Textual Criticism*, 27, among many examples. One may compare a statement of A. E. Housman: "Providence played the editors of Ovid a cruel trick; it put into their hands a 'best MS,' and this was giving gunpowder to a child." The reviewer quoting this adds, "But Housman admits . . . that some MSS are better than others" (cited in Georg Luck, "Textual Criticism Today," *American Journal of Philology* 102 [1981]: 169). Luck also cites the *Encyclopaedia Britannica* article on Housman: "He led the attack on superstitious fidelity to the 'best manuscript' and 'paleographical probability'" (167). Can Housman be invoked on the former point and not also the latter?

73. Aland and Aland, *Text of the New Testament*, 26–30. Other comparisons showing similar results are reported in my "Twentieth-Century Interlude," 387–90 (= *STM* 84–86). Incidentally, the Alands make a further claim (24), that NA²⁷ "comes closer to the original text of the New Testament than did Tischendorf or Westcott and Hort, not to mention von Soden."

74. Aland and Aland, *Text of the New Testament*, 26.

Bernhard Weiss's edition for the third, which tended to rely on Codex Vaticanus (as did WH).[75] This purely mechanical procedure was maintained when Erwin Nestle became editor; his more distinctive contribution was the substantial expansion of the apparatus, albeit by drawing the readings from published editions rather than from manuscripts—and he did so with an extremely high degree of accuracy.[76] After Kurt Aland succeeded to the editorship of NA, readings increasingly were verified from primary sources—the manuscripts themselves.

It may surprise many to learn that, over a period of eighty years, these Nestle and NA texts (through the twenty-fifth edition) "remained the same (apart from a few minor changes adopted by Erwin Nestle—no more than a dozen at most),"[77] and therefore also maintained their same closeness to WH. Yet, as noted above, NA[26] and now NA[27] (with the UBS equivalent texts) still remained closer to WH than to other editions, in spite of the striking fact that in the deliberations over UBS[2] (1968) "the editorial committee (or more precisely its majority) decided to abandon the theories of Westcott-Hort and the 'Western non-interpolations.'"[78] Moreover, we are informed by the preface of UBS[3] (1975) that "more than five hundred changes" were made over against the second edition,[79] and still the closeness to WH remained.

Is there a reasonable explanation for this anomaly? One possible answer may be worthy of suggestion—though no proof is possible—namely, that our modern solidarity in supporting an almost universally adopted critical text may represent a kind of unintentioned and almost unconscious consensus in what we, during the last century and now, are able to reconstruct as our earliest and preferable text of the New Testament. It is almost as if a generally WH-kind of text is a "default position," a dormant text that rises to the surface time and again no matter what tex-

75. Ibid.
76. Ibid., 20–22.
77. Ibid., 26.
78. Ibid., 33. The editorial committees for NA[26] and UBS[3] and for NA[27] and UBS[4] were each composed of the same scholars.
79. UBS[3] viii; also quoted in Aland and Aland, *Text of the New Testament*, 33.

tual scholars do. The late classical textual critic at Johns Hop-
kins University, Georg Luck, said a couple of decades ago that
"our critical texts are no better than our textual critics."[80] Earlier I had taken this statement as an indictment of the discipline,
but I now prefer to interpret it as a compliment to us in the field
of New Testament—because we are doing the very best we can
given our complex situation, even though the result is a compromise. That recognition, however, is neither to invalidate my ca-
reer-long appeal for refining our arguments for the priority of
readings and for clarifying our history of the text, nor is it to re-
nounce an urgent plea that refined methods be utilized in the
improvement of our critical editions—whatever that might
mean. The Alands in their 1989 manual assert that "any further
development of the text must begin from Nestle-Aland[26]. It remains to be seen what the next developments will be." I can
readily accept this statement, but we cannot, I think, accede to
what follows: "Rash decisions should always be avoided. Many
will undoubtedly feel strongly inclined to improve it [the NA
text] here and there. This temptation should be resisted."[81]

Certainly part of the reason for this reluctance to change the
current text is that recently the Münster Institute for New Testament Textual Research, founded by Kurt Aland and now under
the competent leadership of Barbara Aland, has published the
first fascicles of its long awaited *editio critica maior*—a new critical text and extensive apparatus that has received critical ac-
claim for its clear presentation and meticulous care.[82] Although
this first installment of text, containing James, diverges from the

80. Luck, "Textual Criticism Today," 166.
81. Aland and Aland, *Text of the New Testament*, 35–36. NA[27] has the same
text as NA[26], though the apparatus is different. The introduction to NA[27] car-
ries a similar statement, though not with the same thrust: "It should naturally
be understood that this text is a working text (in the sense of the century-long
Nestle tradition): it is not to be considered as definitive, but as a stimulus to
further efforts toward defining and verifying the text of the New Testament.
For many reasons, however, the present edition has not been deemed an appropriate occasion for introducing textual changes" (45*). By contrast, the
preface to UBS[4] (vi) invites readers to submit proposals and suggestions.
82. The Institute for New Testament Textual Research: *Novum Testamentum Graecum, Editio Critica Maior*, vol. 4/1: *Catholic Letters: James* (ed. B.
Aland, K. Aland, G. Mink, and K. Wachtel; Stuttgart: Deutsche Bibelgesellschaft, 1997). Vol. 4/2: *Catholic Letters: The Letters of Peter* appeared in 2000.

NA[27]/UBS[4] text twice, there is an understandable interest in retaining a measure of stability in our commonly used text. At the same time, however, scholars cannot—and will not—be deterred in their calling, and textual critics may be fully expected to continue publishing their proposals for revisions of readings in the NA/UBS text.

Also rather recently, the so-called International Greek New Testament Project has published the papyri of the Gospel of John and continues to work on a full apparatus of that Gospel.[83] A recent and fortunate breakthrough has brought about close cooperation between the Münster Institute and the International Greek New Testament Project after a half-century as separate projects,[84] and the future is much brighter because of these efforts—though achievements in creating critical editions and apparatuses are slow even in the best of circumstances.

So, we ask, finally, whether our current critical text of the Greek New Testament—and there is really only one—reflects a reasonable approximation to the text (or, better, a text) extant in very early Christianity. Unfortunately, we hear two or three answers, which sound quite different: "Yes, we have the original text," and "No, but we have the earliest attainable text." What is anomalous and yet fortunate is that both of these viewpoints, by compromise, can embrace the same general text and continue their labors for progressive improvement as we continue our work in the twenty-first century. A third answer may be, "No, but we have the internal criteria to create it out of the commonly used text"—again a text that appears to be accepted, by compromise, as a working basis. In all of this, however, I still have a lingering question: In view of the numerous, rich discoveries since WH, shouldn't we have been able to produce something better and perhaps very different? The response appears to be the proverbial saying, "The more things change, the more they stay the same"—but that is no answer after all.

---

83. The International Greek New Testament Project: *The New Testament in Greek*, vol. 4/1: *The Gospel according to St. John: The Papyri* (ed. W. J. Elliott and D. C. Parker; New Testament Tools and Studies 20; Leiden: Brill, 1995).

84. E. J. Epp, "The International Greek New Testament Project: Motivation and History," *Novum Testamentum* 39 (1997): 1–20.

Choosing to Address Context—and Deciding on Influence: The Issue of Manuscripts and Variant Readings in Their Church-Historical, Cultural, and Intellectual Contexts

New Testament textual criticism is far broader and richer than mere arguments for priority of readings, proposals about text-types, and the construction of critical texts and apparatuses. The contexts in which manuscripts and variant readings are found and used, as well as the contexts in which we choose to examine them, illumine for us the history and thought of the church, both in the early period and later. In approaching these contexts, it is relevant to note that each of the issues treated earlier has a lengthy history: critical editions reach back to the early sixteenth century, and canons of criticism and text-types to the early eighteenth century, though all three received major attention in the twentieth century. Much less attention, however, was afforded the present issue in the late nineteenth and early twentieth centuries—the influence of the church and its theology on the manuscripts and variants of the New Testament text and the reverse, the influence of the text on the church. In addition, we extend this issue to include the cultural and intellectual context of our New Testament manuscripts.

Textual Criticism and Early Church History

With a few notable exceptions, the relationship of textual criticism and the theology of the church was much neglected in the second half of the twentieth century—until very recently. Already in 1904, however, Kirsopp Lake urged textual critics to examine variants as a window on exegesis in the church: "We need to know," he said, "what the early Church thought [a passage] meant and how it altered its wording in order to emphasize its meaning."[85] Two decades earlier Hort had alerted textual critics to the issue, though in a negative fashion, by his frequently quoted statement of 1882 that in the New Testament "there are no signs of deliberate falsifica-

85. K. Lake, *The Influence of Textual Criticism on the Exegesis of the New Testament: An Inaugural Lecture Delivered before the University of Leiden, on January 27, 1904* (Oxford: Parker, 1904), 12.

tion of the text for dogmatic purposes" (WH 2:282-83; cf. "Notes on Select Readings" in WH 2:64-69). In his continuing discussion, he allows one exception: the "wilful tampering with the text" by Marcion,· the first declared heretic in the church. Curiously, Hort's view was first "refuted" by Dean Burgon and Edward Miller by their accusations of intentional corruption in the old uncial manuscripts—part of their defense of the *textus receptus* (see n. 74 above). Other scholars, more enlightened in their criticism of Hort, pointed to anti-Jewish intrusions into the text or suggested textual variants showing the influence of additional heretics, such as Montanus, particularly in the D-text.[86] J. Rendel Harris argued the latter and, more generally along the lines of Lake, urged that the history of the text be read side by side with second-century church history and in view of various parties in it.[87] Indeed, in 1914, Harris, recalling the famous dictum of Hort that "knowledge of documents should precede final judgement upon readings" (WH 2:31), sharpened the issue succinctly by adding that "knowledge . . . of Church History should precede final judgment as to readings."[88] By 1926, however, James Hardy Ropes, who edited the D-text of Acts, drew a conclusion clear to him: "Of any special point of view, theological or other, on the part of the 'Western' reviser it is difficult to find any trace."[89] Actually, it was this sentence by Ropes that provided the challenge for my 1966 investigation of anti-Judaic tendencies in the D-text of Acts, which attempted on a large scale to place the variant readings of that early textual tradition in an ideological/theological context.[90] Previously, little had been done to identify theologically motivated textual variants in a systematic fashion throughout a

---

86. Summary in E. J. Epp, *The Theological Tendency of Codex Bezae Cantabrigiensis in Acts* (Society for New Testament Studies Monograph 3; Cambridge: Cambridge University Press, 1966), 2-4, 15.

87. J. R. Harris, untitled introduction in *Bulletin of the Bezan Club* 6 (1929): 2; idem, "New Points of View in Textual Criticism," *Expositor* 8 (1914): 322.

88. Harris, "New Points of View," 322.

89. J. H. Ropes, *The Text of Acts* (vol. 3 of *The Beginnings of Christianity: The Acts of the Apostles*; ed. F. J. Foakes Jackson and K. Lake; London: Macmillan, 1926), ccxxxiii.

90. See Epp, *Theological Tendency of Codex Bezae.*

text-type in a lengthy New Testament book, and the Book of Acts was an eminently appropriate place to attempt it because of its dual-stream textual tradition. I found that challenge heightened by a view of New Testament textual criticism that emerged from the University of Chicago in the years just before and after World War II, a view that is well summarized by a single paragraph from Donald W. Riddle:

> The legitimate task of textual criticism is not limited to the recovery of approximately the original form of the documents, to the establishment of the "best" text, nor to the "elimination of spurious readings." It must be recognized that every significant variant records a religious experience which brought it into being. This means that there are no "spurious readings": the various forms of the text are sources for the study of the history of Christianity.[91]

Later, his colleague, Merrill M. Parvis, picked up on the words *spurious readings*:

> All are part of the tradition; all contribute to our knowledge of the history of Christian thought. And they are significant contributions because they are interpretations which were highly enough thought of in some place and at some time to be incorporated into the Scripture itself.[92]

In the same year, Ernest C. Colwell, soon to be recognized as a brilliant text-critical methodologist, wrote, "Most variations . . . were made deliberately" and "the majority of the variant readings in the New Testament were created for theological or dogmatic reasons." In the same context, Colwell added "It was because they [the books of the New Testament] were the religious treasure of the church that they were changed" and

> The paradox is that the variations came into existence because they were religious books, sacred books, canonical books. The

91. D. W. Riddle, "Textual Criticism as a Historical Discipline," *Anglican Theological Review* 18 (1936): 221.

92. M. M. Parvis, "The Nature and Tasks of New Testament Textual Criticism: An Appraisal," *Journal of Religion* 32 (1952): 172.

devout scribe felt compelled to correct misstatements which he found in the manuscripts he was copying.[93]

(Of course, neither Colwell nor his colleagues were speaking of obvious scribal errors.)

In 1966 I described this Chicago view as "Present-Day Textual Criticism,"[94] but, as I wrote elsewhere recently,[95] I was overly optimistic by a quarter of a century and more, for only the recent works of Bart Ehrman and David Parker have brought that general approach into currency.

Ehrman, in his *Orthodox Corruption of Scripture*, for example, demonstrates more than adequately that numerous textual variations were fostered by those supporting orthodox theological views (in surprising contrast to the view at the turn of the last century that only heretics could be accused of such behavior).[96] Though it is trite to say it, obviously not all of Ehrman's examples are persuasive, but clearly he has made his point that, in various ways in the second and third centuries, proto-orthodox scribes (as he calls them) "modified their texts of scripture in light of the polemical contexts within which they worked, altering the manuscripts they reproduced to make them more orthodox on the one hand and less susceptible to heretics on the other."[97] To what church-historical context does he refer? He points to the christological controversies in the first centuries of Christianity and specifically to three groups that resisted the emerging orthodoxy: adoptionists, docetists, and separationists.

93. E. C. Colwell, *What Is the Best New Testament?* (Chicago: University of Chicago Press, 1952), 52–53. He also states: "The importance of the Book in their religious life led them to 'correct' the mistakes. Unfortunately, they thought they knew more than they actually did, and thus, with the best intentions in the world, they corrupted the text of the New Testament" (53). Cf. this with the view of Ehrman, discussed below.

94. Epp, *Theological Tendency of Codex Bezae*, 12–21.

95. E. J. Epp, "The Multivalence of the Term 'Original Text' in New Testament Textual Criticism," *Harvard Theological Review* 92 (1999): 271–72.

96. B. D. Ehrman, *The Orthodox Corruption of Scripture: The Effect of Early Christological Controversies on the Text of the New Testament* (New York: Oxford University Press, 1993); cf. idem, "The Text as Window: New Testament Manuscripts and the Social History of Early Christianity," in *TNTCR* 361–79.

97. Ehrman, *Orthodox Corruption of Scripture*, 15; cf. 275.

Ehrman enlightens us further about scribal mentality in such a setting. As scribes introduced intentional changes into the writings that were to become the New Testament, they would "make them *say* what they were already known to *mean*,"[98] thus "corrupting" their texts for theological reasons in support of the emerging mainstream theology of the time, that is, orthodoxy (which accounts for the title of his book). Clearly scribes such as these acted with noble motivation and were compelled by conviction. Ehrman's own summary at the very end of his book describes his view concisely:

> Understanding a text . . . involves putting it "in other words." Anyone who explains a text "in other words," however, has altered the words.
> This is exactly what the scribes did: they occasionally altered the words of the text by putting them "in other words." To this extent, they were textual interpreters. At the same time, by *physically* altering the words, they did something quite different from other exegetes, and this difference is by no means to be minimized. Whereas all readers change a text when they construe it in their minds, the scribes actually changed the text on the page. As a result, they created a new text . . . over which future interpreters would dispute, no longer having access to the words of the original text, the words produced by the author.[99]

In a subsequent article, Ehrman directs his analysis to textual variants that reveal broader sociocultural issues in the early church, such as Jewish-Christian relations, attitudes toward women, and even the use of New Testament manuscripts to foretell the future.[100] So, Ehrman, in several ways, spells out in detail what Kirsopp Lake sought from textual critics nearly ninety years ago: to know what the early church thought a passage meant and how it altered its wording to emphasize its meaning, and also what Rendel Harris recommended, namely, reading textual criticism side by side with church history. As William Petersen puts it, Ehrman's book "demonstrates once

98. Ibid., xii (emphasis in original).
99. Ibid., 280 (emphasis in original).
100. Ehrman, "Text as Window." Note the references to recent work by others in these and additional areas.

again that the most reliable guide to the development of Christian theology is the ever-changing text of the New Testament."[101] By way of summary, textual variants that disclose theological thought, doctrinal controversy, and other sociocultural attitudes and practices become (to use Ehrman's phrase in the title of his essay "The Text as Window") a window that enlarges our vista on early Christianity, enriching, confirming, and correcting our conception of that crucial period of church history.

Four years after Ehrman's work, a disarmingly small volume appeared, *The Living Text of the Gospels* by David Parker.[102] His views arose primarily from consideration of important cases in the manuscript tradition where the readings in a variation unit are multiple and do not yield an easily determined original reading or any plausible original at all. Confronted with numerous such bundles of textual variants, Parker describes the text of the four Gospels as one that from the beginning grew freely,[103] for "sayings and stories continued to be developed by copyists and readers."[104] He reaffirms what textual critics generally hold, that the most dramatic changes in the text occurred in the first 150 years, leading him to describe the Gospel text "as a free, or perhaps as a living, text,"[105] which accounts for the title of his book. The Gospels are "not archives of traditions but living texts,"[106] and, therefore, he says bluntly, "The concept of a Gospel that is fixed in shape, authoritative, and final as a piece of literature has to be abandoned."[107] When we ask what church-historical context Parker is invoking here, it is this: "The [free] text indicates that to at least some early Christians, it was more important to hand on the spirit of Jesus' teaching than to remember the letter. . . . The material about Jesus was preserved in an interpretive rather than an exact fashion."[108]

101. W. L. Petersen, review of B. D. Ehrman's *Orthodox Corruption of Scripture, Journal of Religion* 74 (1994): 563–64.
102. D. C. Parker, *The Living Text of the Gospels* (Cambridge: Cambridge University Press, 1997).
103. Ibid., 203.
104. Ibid., 45–46.
105. Ibid., 200.
106. Ibid., 119.
107. Ibid., 93.
108. D. C. Parker, "Scripture Is Tradition," *Theology* 94 (1991): 15.

I can refer to only one of Parker's extended examples, with brief reference to one or two others. When Parker, an accomplished textual critic, surveys the array of variant readings that accompany the Gospel sayings on marriage and divorce, he is compelled to conclude that, in this case, "the recovery of a single original saying of Jesus is impossible"; rather, "what we have here is a collection of interpretive rewritings of a tradition":[109] "The early church rewrote the sayings in their attempt to make sense of them."[110] So, when Parker says that "the Gospel texts exist only as a manuscript tradition"[111] and not in an early, fixed form, he means to apply that statement to both the past and present, allowing the richness of the manuscripts, with all of their variants and with the interpretations and insights that they offer, to illuminate not only the culture of the early church but of today as well. In other words, the full manuscript tradition in a given variation unit provides us today vastly more than if we were limited to a single original reading or text. Yet, this does not mean that all variants on divorce, for example, now have the authority traditionally ascribed only to one of those readings. "The tradition is manifold. . . . There is no authoritative text beyond the manuscripts which we may follow without further thought"; hence, says Parker, "The people of God have to make up their own minds. There is no authoritative text to provide a short-cut."[112]

This is the intriguing new direction in which Parker pulls New Testament textual criticism—making a virtue out of complex and often insoluble text-critical cruxes by showing, first, how they cast light on both routine and controversial issues in the early church and, second, how they still have practical relevance for the church today. Some surely will see his view as a negative move, but I join Parker in claiming the positive side. He remarks that "the church came into being . . . as the community of the Spirit," but the tradition of this community is manifold, including both oral and written forms. Yet, that tradition

109. Parker, *Living Text of the Gospels*, 92–93.
110. Ibid., 183.
111. Ibid., 203.
112. Ibid., 212.

has come down to us only in manuscripts with multiple texts
and readings:

> Rather than looking for right and wrong readings, and with
> them for right or wrong beliefs and practices, the way is open
> for the possibility that the church is the community of the
> Spirit even in its multiplicities of texts. . . . Indeed, we may sug-
> gest that it is not in spite of the variety but because of them that
> the church is that community.[113]

Hence, as Parker views it, we actually find ourselves in a favor-
able situation: "Who before in the history of theological thought
has had access to the text of dozens of early manuscripts? More
than at any other time, we are able to see how the tradition developed"[114]—that is, the multiple variants permit us to be part of the
discussions and controversies—indeed, the very life—of the early
church as they agonized over certain difficult issues, allowing us
to understand, for example, that there was not only one interpretation, prescription, or practice of marriage and divorce, nor was
there a unitary view of other crucial matters. From this, Parker
draws a far-reaching conclusion about the task of textual criticism, which, he says, has "long accepted the role that has been
demanded of it as provider of authoritative text."[115] While the
discipline need not give up its more traditional goals,[116] this new
perspective broadens and enriches the tasks of textual criticism
by showing how variants both were influenced by situations in
the church and, in turn, influenced church thought and practice—and (a major point for Parker) they retain the power to do
so today. In the marriage/divorce case, for example, "we find that
the saying(s) of Jesus on this subject had, as one might say, a life
of their own,"[117] and this rich multitextual tradition is still available for our instruction. Lest it be thought that such a view had
no precedent, notice that Origen (died 254) was "able to make

113. Ibid.
114. Ibid., 93.
115. Ibid., 94.
116. See Parker's views on seeking the original text (ibid., 132–37, 211; also
182, 209), but see the discussion below on goals and directions versus meanings and approaches.
117. Ibid., 94.

both readings [in Hebrews 2:9] yield edifying truths" and, in another instance (Matthew 18:1), after mentioning two variant readings "it makes no difference which reading is original, and he expresses no opinion on the matter."[118] When Parker examines another case where myriad variant readings occur, the (so-called) Lord's Prayer, he finds (as textual critics well know) six main forms in the tangled manuscript tradition:

> All six forms contribute to our understanding. Once we have discovered their existence, they will be part of the way in which we read and interpret the Lord's Prayer. We shall not be able to erase them from our minds, and to read a single original text as though the others had never existed.[119]

Again, the church has been in the past and continues to be instructed by all meaningful multiple variants since they disclose how the early church dealt with or thought about theological or ethical issues and about worship. Indeed, permit me to add a paradoxical statement of my own: *the greater the ambiguity in the variant readings in a given variation unit, the more clearly we are able to grasp the concerns of the early church.* If that is a fair paraphrase of Parker's viewpoint (and I think it is), we have fascinating, profound, and enlarged parameters for text-critical studies in the present century.

Parker later treats the last three chapters of Luke as a whole and finds that variants in 40 of the last 167 verses in that Gospel provide, as he says, "incontrovertible evidence that the text of these chapters was not fixed, and indeed continued to grow for centuries after its composition,"[120] including "a significant number of passages which were added to the Gospel in order to emphasize its orthodoxy."[121] "We might say," he concludes (in a memorable statement), "that Luke is not, in these early centuries, a closed book. It is open, and successive generations write on its pages."[122]

---

118. For details, see Metzger, "Practice of Textual Criticism among the Church Fathers," 342–43.
119. Parker, *Living Text of the Gospels*, 102.
120. Ibid., 172.
121. Ibid., 183.
122. Ibid., 174.

We see now how Parker's analysis and his bold statements and Ehrman's creative position reconnect us with the views of Lake, Harris, and the Chicago school and—it should be noted— meet the complaint of the Alands that "New Testament textual criticism has traditionally neglected the findings of early Church history, but only to its own injury."[123] Now we have new possibilities in this important arena, with the goals of textual criticism properly expanded as well.

New Testament Manuscripts in Their Cultural, Intellectual Context

A very different approach to context in New Testament textual criticism involves placing manuscripts in their contemporary setting. Regrettably, this is a subject in which there are many questions and few answers; any answers, however, that can be found will assist in the writing of the history of the New Testament text. Hence, the effort is well worthwhile. The most obviously relevant area is the provenance of manuscripts, which, in its simplest form, provides known places of origin of individual manuscripts that can be used to explain and illumine the distinctive or characteristic readings of each manuscript and, more broadly, to place each manuscript within the history of the text. Thus, a manuscript from Egypt or Caesarea or Constantinople may be expected to reflect its context—its brand of Christianity in its period. Of course, the difficulties and complexities are great: for instance, a manuscript from a known locality may reflect, rather, the context of its exemplar, whose provenance is unknown, or a manuscript may have been found in one locality, such as Egypt, but may have been written elsewhere and brought to Egypt.

The greatest obstacle, however, is that the provenance of most of our important New Testament manuscripts is debated or simply unknown, undoubtedly depriving us of much useful information.[124] For example, among the notable

---

123. Aland and Aland, *Text of the New Testament*, 49; cf. 52.
124. For a summary, see E. J. Epp, "The New Testament Papyri at Oxyrhynchus in Their Social and Intellectual Context," in *Sayings of Jesus: Canonical and Non-canonical: Essays in Honour of Tjitze Baarda* (ed. W. L. Petersen, J. S. Vos, and H. J. de Jonge; Novum Testamentum Supplement 89; Leiden: Brill, 1997), 50–51.

fourth- and fifth-century parchment codices, it has long been suggested that the two most famous ones, Vaticanus and Sinaiticus, were among the fifty parchment manuscripts that Eusebius says were ordered by Constantine (around 331) for new churches in Constantinople;[125] others, however, think Vaticanus could have originated in Egypt (Lake), or specifically Alexandria (Birdsall), or Caesarea (Milne and Skeat).[126] As for Codex Alexandrinus (A), its origin is usually assumed to have been Alexandria, but it might have come from Constantinople, Caesarea, or Beirut.[127] David Parker, in his meticulous monograph on Codex Bezae (D), dismisses nine proposals for its place of origin and opts for Beirut, though more recently Allen Callahan argues, once again, for an Egyptian origin.[128] And H. A. Sanders furnishes evidence that Codex Washingtonianus (W) was found near a ruined monastery near Giza.[129] Yet, virtually all of these designations fall short of demonstration.

When we ask about the New Testament papyri, the Chester Beatty manuscripts ($\mathfrak{P}^{45}$, $\mathfrak{P}^{46}$, $\mathfrak{P}^{47}$), at the time of their purchase about 1930, were reported to have been discovered near

125. Based on Eusebius's reference (*Life of Constantine* 4.36) to "volumes of threefold and fourfold forms," a tenuous but perhaps plausible way of describing the three- and four-column formats, respectively, of these two grand codices; see Metzger, *Text of the New Testament*, 7–8.

126. See now T. C. Skeat, "The Codex Sinaiticus, the Codex Vaticanus and Constantine," *Journal of Theological Studies* 50 (1999): 583–625, esp. 598–604; see also J. N. Birdsall, "The New Testament Text," in *The Cambridge History of the Bible*, vol. 1: *From the Beginnings to Jerome* (ed. P. R. Ackroyd and C. F. Evans; Cambridge: Cambridge University Press, 1970), 359–60; Metzger, *Text of the New Testament*, 7–8.

127. Streeter, *Four Gospels*, 120 n. 1.

128. D. C. Parker, *Codex Bezae: An Early Christian Manuscript and Its Text* (Cambridge: Cambridge University Press, 1992), 261–78. A. D. Callahan ("Again: The Origin of Codex Bezae," in *Codex Bezae: Studies from the Lunel Colloquium, June 1994* [ed. D. C. Parker and C.-B. Amphoux; New Testament Tools and Studies 22; Leiden: Brill, 1996], 56–64) proposes as the scribe of Codex Bezae a native Egyptian whose mother tongue was Subachmimic Coptic and who "neither spoke nor wrote either Greek or Latin with scholarly proficiency" (63–64).

129. H. A. Sanders, *The New Testament Manuscripts in the Freer Collection*, vol. 1: *The Washington Manuscript of the Four Gospels* (University of Michigan Studies: Humanistic Series 9; New York: Macmillan, 1912), 1–4. He refers to the Monastery of the Vinedresser.

Atfih (Aphroditopolis) in the Fayûm,[130] while $\mathfrak{P}^{52}$, still considered the earliest New Testament manuscript, was assumed to have come from the Fayûm or Oxyrhynchus.[131] Again, certainty of provenance is elusive. More recently James M. Robinson identifies the Bodmer Papyri with the Dishna Papers, discovered near Dishnā in Upper Egypt, east of Nag Hammadi; the collection included $\mathfrak{P}^{66}$, $\mathfrak{P}^{72}$, $\mathfrak{P}^{75}$, and $\mathfrak{P}^{99}$ (though not $\mathfrak{P}^{74}$), which were part of the nearby Pachomian monastic library until they were buried in a large earthen jar, probably in the seventh century. Robinson concludes, however, that these three early New Testament papyri, which antedate the founding of that monastic order (in the early fourth century), came from elsewhere.[132] Thus, the ultimate origin of $\mathfrak{P}^{66}$, $\mathfrak{P}^{72}$, $\mathfrak{P}^{75}$, and $\mathfrak{P}^{99}$ still eludes us.

We have more precise information on about two dozen other papyri: $\mathfrak{P}^{4}$ (third century) containing Luke was found *in situ* in Coptos (= Qift, about 250 miles up the Nile from Oxyrhynchus) in a jar walled up in a house; the papyrus had been utilized in the binding of a (presumably Christian) codex of Philo, though the house showed no evident connection to a church. $\mathfrak{P}^{92}$ (third/fourth century) turned up at Madînat Mâdî (modern Narmouthis, in the Fayûm) in a rubble-filled structure near a racecourse. $\mathfrak{P}^{40}$ (third century) was discovered at Qarara in Middle Egypt, only about ten miles down the Nile from Oxyrhynchus, while $\mathfrak{P}^{43}$ (sixth/seventh century) turned up in a sixth-/seventh-century monastic settlement at Wadi Sarga (fifteen miles south

---

130. C. H. Roberts, *Manuscript, Society and Belief in Early Christian Egypt* (Schweich Lectures 1977; London: Oxford University Press for the British Academy, 1979), 7.

131. C. H. Roberts, *An Unpublished Fragment of the Fourth Gospel in the John Rylands Library* (Manchester: Manchester University Press, 1935), 24–25; H. I. Bell and T. C. Skeat, *Fragments of an Unknown Gospel and Other Early Christian Papyri* (London: British Museum, 1935), 7.

132. J. M. Robinson, *The Pachomian Monastic Library at the Chester Beatty Library and the Bibliothèque Bodmer* (Occasional Papers 19; Claremont, Calif.: Institute for Antiquity and Christianity, 1990), esp. 4–6, 22–26. A shorter version of this work appeared as "The First Christian Monastic Library," in *Coptic Studies: Acts of the Third International Congress of Coptic Studies, Warsaw, 20–25 August 1984* (ed. W. Godlewski; Centre d'archéologie méditerranéenne de l'Académie Polonaise des Sciences; Warsaw: Éditions scientifiques de Pologne, 1990), 371–78.

of Asyut). Nine other papyri were found at various sites in the Fayûm ($\mathfrak{P}^3$, $\mathfrak{P}^{12}$, $\mathfrak{P}^{33+58}$, $\mathfrak{P}^{34}$, $\mathfrak{P}^{53}$, $\mathfrak{P}^{55}$, $\mathfrak{P}^{56}$, $\mathfrak{P}^{57}$, $\mathfrak{P}^{79}$) and one at Thebes ($\mathfrak{P}^{44}$). Outside Egypt, several were discovered in the Negeb ($\mathfrak{P}^{59}$, $\mathfrak{P}^{60}$, and $\mathfrak{P}^{61}$ at ʿAuja-el-Hafir [ancient Nessana] in a collapsed room annexed to a small church; and $\mathfrak{P}^{11}$, $\mathfrak{P}^{14}$, and $\mathfrak{P}^{68}$ at Sinai) and two more at Khirbet Mird in a ruined Christian monastery on the site of the earlier fortress, Hyrcania, near the Dead Sea in Judea ($\mathfrak{P}^{83}$, $\mathfrak{P}^{84}$).[133]

All such information is to be valued, though it is not yet clear exactly how this sort of discrete information might assist us. About all we can say at this juncture is that something is known of the provenance of these thirty New Testament papyri but almost nothing of some thirty-six others. There remains, however, one large group of manuscripts whose provenance is certain, or at least their place of use and discovery is indisputable (thus allowing for the possibility that some among them may have originated elsewhere). That group consists of the papyri (and majuscule fragments) discovered in the rubbish heaps and deserted houses at Oxyrhynchus in Egypt, some two hundred miles up the Nile from Alexandria. At this site, 47 (or 42%) of our 112 different New Testament papyri were discovered (116 is the numbered total to date),[134] and collectively they contain portions of fifteen New Testament books. More striking is the fact that among the 61 earliest New Testament manuscripts (those dating up to and around the turn of the third/fourth centuries), 35 (or 57%) come from Oxyrhynchus.

133. On $\mathfrak{P}^4$, see Roberts, *Manuscript, Society and Belief*, 8, 13; on $\mathfrak{P}^{92}$, see C. Gallazzi, "Frammenti di un codice con le Epistole di Paoli," *Zeitschrift für Papyrologie und Epigraphik* 46 (1982): 117; on $\mathfrak{P}^{43}$, see W. E. Crum and H. I. Bell (eds.), *Wadi Sarga: Coptic and Greek Texts from the Excavations Undertaken by the Byzantine Research Account* (Hauniae: Gyldenalske Boghandel, 1922), 43–45; cf. 29–45; on $\mathfrak{P}^{59}$, $\mathfrak{P}^{60}$, and $\mathfrak{P}^{61}$, see Jack Finegan, *Encountering New Testament Manuscripts* (Grand Rapids: Eerdmans, 1974), 94–100. For the place of discovery—whenever known—of New Testament papyri through $\mathfrak{P}^{88}$, see K. Aland, *Repertorium der griechischen christlichen Papyri*, vol. 1: *Biblische Papyri* (Patristische Texte und Studien 18; Berlin: de Gruyter, 1976), 215–322.

134. For $\mathfrak{P}^{116}$ (sixth or seventh century), containing portions of Hebrews 2:9–11 and 3:3–6, see A. Papathomas, "A New Testmony to the Letter to the Hebrews," *Journal of Greco-Roman Christianity and Judaism* 1 (2000): 18–24.

Such data thrust these 47 Oxyrhynchus papyri of known provenance into a unique position, offering an unparalleled opportunity for New Testament textual criticism to assess a large number of copies of Christianity's earliest writings within the literary and intellectual environment of a single location. Many thousands of other papyrus documents have been recovered from the same site, including business and official documents, private letters, and literary works, of which more than 4,600 have been published to date in the sixty-seven volumes of *The Oxyrhynchus Papyri*,[135] as well as hundreds elsewhere. These papyri furnish for us the immediate and larger context for the New Testament manuscripts from Oxyrhynchus, for they range across the entire gamut of life and livelihood in Oxyrhynchus, covering education and learning; commerce, agriculture, and transportation; legal transactions and proceedings; politics, government, and the military; cultural, religious, and social life; work and leisure; as well as everyday events such as marriage and divorce, child rearing, family joys and sorrows, health and sickness, and natural disasters. I cannot review here either this wealth of material or my own research on it, though I would like to present five private letters from everyday life in Oxyrhynchus and then offer a brief description of the city.

In the third century, a boy away at school writes his father at Oxyrhynchus:

> Now do not be uneasy, father, about my studies; I am working hard and taking relaxation; I shall do well. (third century C.E.; P.Oxy. 10:1296; Loeb Classical Library 1:137)

About the same time, another son throws a tantrum in a letter to his father, but changes his tone near the end of the letter:

> Theon to . . . his father, greeting. You did a fine thing; you didn't take me with you to the city. If you do not wish to take me with you to Alexandria, I'll not write you a letter or talk to you or wish you good health. What's more, if you go to Alexandria, I won't shake your hand or greet you again. So if you do not wish to take me with you, that's that! . . . But you did a fine thing; you sent me presents, big ones, [bean] pods! . . . But send for

---

135. *The Oxyrhynchus Papyri* (67 vols. to date; Graeco-Roman Memoirs; London: Egypt Exploration Society for the British Academy, 1898–).

me, I beg you. If you do not send, I won't eat, won't drink!
There! I pray for your good health. (second or third century
C.E.; P.Oxy. 1:119)[136]

Just about the time of Jesus' birth, a husband writes this disturbing letter to his wife:

> Know that I am still in Alexandria. . . . I ask and beg you to take
> good care of our baby son, and as soon as I receive payment I
> will send it up to you. If you are delivered of child [before I get
> home], if it is a boy keep it, if a girl discard [expose] it. You
> have sent me word, "Don't forget me." How can I forget you? I
> beg you not to worry. (17 June 1 B.C.E.; P.Oxy. 4:744)[137]

A man in some unknown distress in the fourth century sends
this impassioned plea for help, which is surprisingly philo-
sophical:

> Hermias to his sister, greeting. What remains to write to you
> about I do not know, for I have told you of everything till I am
> tired, and yet you pay no attention. When a man finds himself
> in adversity he ought to give way and not fight stubbornly
> against fate. We fail to realize the inferiority and wretchedness
> to which we are born. Well, so far nothing at all has been done;
> make it your business to send some one to me . . . to stay with
> me until I know the position of my affairs. Am I to be . . .
> oppressed until Heaven takes pity on me? . . . See that matters
> are properly conducted on your own part, or our disasters will
> be complete. We are resolved not to continue in misfortune.
> Farewell; I wish you all prosperity.

On the reverse side, he pleads again:

> Whatever you do, do not fail me in my trouble. . . . Can time
> accomplish everything after all? (fourth century C.E.; P.Oxy.
> 1:120; Loeb Classical Library 1:162)

136. Translation from J. G. Winter, *Life and Letters in the Papyri* (Jerome
Lectures; Ann Arbor: University of Michigan Press, 1933), 60.
137. Translation from N. Lewis, *Life in Egypt under Roman Rule* (Oxford:
Clarendon, 1983), 54; cf. Loeb Classical Library 1:105. Fortunately, Egyptian
religion forbade exposure of children, and they were often rescued from the
dung heaps, as we learn from other Oxyrhynchus papyri.

Finally, another unknown calamity prompts a defiant threat even to the gods:

> To Stephanus from Hephaestion. On the receipt of the letter . . . put off everything and come at once to the homestead because of what has happened to me. If you take no heed, as the gods have not spared me, so will I not spare the gods. Goodbye. (third century C.E.; P.Oxy. 7:1065; Loeb Classical Library 1:138)

Apart from these reflections of everyday events and emotions, what was Oxyrhynchus like? The papyri from the period 30 B.C.E.–96 C.E. alone provide us with some fifty-seven hundred names of residents in this district capital, which had a population of perhaps thirty thousand in Roman times, a figure based on the ruins of a theater that seated between eight thousand and twelve thousand.[138] Oxyrhynchus also had some twenty temples,[139] at least two churches (P.Oxy. 1:43 verso; 295 C.E.), and a Jewish synagogue (P.Oxy. 9:1205; 291 C.E.) around the turn of the third/fourth centuries. It is of interest that the synagogue paid fourteen talents of silver (a large sum) to free a woman and her two small children, one of whom was named Jacob.[140] Of course, religion in Oxyrhynchus was dominated by Greek and Roman practices and by the continuance of traditional Egyptian rites, as attested by innumerable references in the papyri to temples, deities, officiants, festivals, and sacrifices, in addition to the inevitable prayers and invocations of the gods in private letters,[141] yet Christianity obviously flourished there as well, for in the early sixth century a bishop, some forty churches, and a

138. On names, see B. W. Jones and J. E. G. Whitehorne, *Register of Oxyrhynchites 30 B.C.–A.D. 96* (American Studies in Papyrology 25; Chico, Calif.: Scholars Press, 1983). On population and the theater, see E. G. Turner, *Greek Papyri: An Introduction* (Oxford: Clarendon, 1968), 81–82. William Petrie, the excavator in 1922, estimated that the theater held 11,200 spectators (see E. G. Turner, "Roman Oxyrhynchus," *Journal of Egyptian Archaeology* 38 [1952]: 81; and J. Krüger, *Oxyrhynchos in der Kaiserzeit: Studien zur Topographie und Literaturrezeption* [European University Studies 3/441; Frankfurt am Main: Lang, 1990], 8).

139. Turner, "Roman Oxyrhynchus," 82–83, provides a list of temples.

140. See P.Oxy. 9:1205 and *Corpus Papyrorum Judaicarum* (ed. V. Tcherikover and A. Fuks; Cambridge: Harvard University Press, 1957), 1:94.

141. See, e.g., Turner, "Roman Oxyrhynchus," 82–83.

calendar of church services are attested by the papyri (P.Oxy. 11:1357; 535–36 c.e.). We even have an early fourth-century letter showing that Christians exchanged books: "To my dearest lady sister, greetings in the Lord. Lend [me] the Ezra, since I lent you the little Genesis. Farewell in God from us" (P.Oxy. 63:4365).

What are more relevant—and more intriguing—for the issue at hand are some seventeen hundred published literary papyri found at Oxyrhynchus, containing fragments as well as substantial portions of classical literature and dating over a seven-hundred-year period (ca. second/first century B.C.E. to sixth/seventh century C.E.). If we count up the manuscripts from the same general period as the early group of New Testament papyri (i.e., to about 325), we encounter, to give a very short list, 42 copies of Euripides, 58 of Plato, 62 of Demosthenes, 72 of Thucydides, 84 of Hesiod, and 234 of Homer. But there is more than classical literature; Jewish and Christian writings (other than the New Testament) are found in some abundance from the period selected. For example, about ten manuscripts containing Jewish Scripture (plus ten more from later in the fourth century) have been published, many of which doubtless were made for Christian use; and we have about twenty-five Christian writings, including ten apocryphal gospels, six apocryphal apocalypses, and various others books (plus nearly twenty more later in the fourth century).[142] Remember, all these writings, as well as the New Testament papyri, represent what the Oxyrhynchites discarded—threw out in their rubbish heaps—perhaps because the volumes were worn out, and we have no way of knowing how many books were in use at a given time or what happened to those that were.

The Oxford Classical Dictionary reports that "over 70 per cent of surviving literary papyri come from Oxyrhynchus,"[143] sug-

142. For more detail, see Epp, "New Testament Papyri at Oxyrhynchus in Their Social and Intellectual Context," 59–62; idem, "The New Testament Papyri at Oxyrhynchus: Their Significance for Understanding the Transmission of the Early New Testament Text," in Oxyrhynchus: A City and Its Texts (centennial volume of The Oxyrhynchus Papyri; London: Egypt Exploration Society for the British Academy, forthcoming).

143. W. E. H. Cockle, "Oxyrhynchus," in The Oxford Classical Dictionary (ed. S. Hornblower and A. Spawforth; 3d ed.; Oxford: Oxford University Press, 1996), 1088.

gesting that this city was exceptional in its possession and use of literature, just as it appears to be exceptional in the number of New Testament writings found there. To count literary works available is not necessarily to say much about literary activity and particularly literary criticism in Oxyrhynchus, but there is abundant evidence in the papyri of a lively literary scene, of the study of literature in the schools, of the procurement and exchange of books, of the active critique of literature, and of intellectual interchange with Alexandria.[144]

Now come the questions. The location within this cultural-intellectual milieu of so high a percentage of our extant New Testament papyri prompts us to ask what impact this kind of community might have had upon Christianity up to the early fourth century—and what Christianity's impact upon Oxyrhynchus might have been. More specifically, what might be the significance for understanding the use, study, and transmission of the New Testament text when 42% of all known New Testament papyri and 57% of the oldest group of manuscripts have spent their useful life in a city with a vibrant intellectual climate, including literary activity in the form of scholarly analysis, criticism, and editing? Does this suggest, for example, that Christians might have engaged in similar scholarly editing of their own literature, including their copies of the Gospels, Paul, and other writings? (I tried to answer this question by testing for some phenomena, namely, whether the Oxyrhynchus New Testament papyri reveal the same kinds of scholar's notations and editor's critical marks that are found with considerable frequency in manuscripts of Homer and the numerous other authors represented at Oxyrhynchus; my preliminary investigations led to a negative answer.)[145] And, somewhat farther afield, what does this intellectual climate in Oxyrhynchus say about lit-

144. For examples and discussion, see Epp, "New Testament Papyri at Oxyrhynchus in Their Social and Intellectual Context," 56–59, 63–66; idem, "The Codex and Literacy in Early Christianity and at Oxyrhynchus: Issues Raised by Harry Y. Gamble's *Books and Readers in the Early Church*," *Critical Review of Books in Religion* 10 (1997): 32–34; idem, "New Testament Papyri at Oxyrhynchus: Their Significance."

145. See Epp, "Codex and Literacy in Early Christianity and at Oxyrhynchus," 30–32; idem, "New Testament Papyri at Oxyrhynchus: Their Significance."

eracy among Oxyrhynchites in general and the Christians there in particular,[146] and what might this all tell us about the size, character, vitality, and influence of the Christian community at Oxyrhynchus and about the nature of early Christianity in Egypt as a whole? Exact answers, of course, are unlikely, but this unique situation must be exploited for anything and everything it can offer. I suggest elsewhere that Oxyrhynchus is a microcosm of the textual spectrum of our New Testament manuscripts,[147] and my fond hope is that in the present century we may find ways in which the Oxyrhynchus New Testament papyri can help us clarify our sketch of the history of the Greek New Testament text.

Choosing to Address Goals and Directions—and Deciding on Meanings and Approaches: The Issue of Original Text

The final current issue actually brings us back, logically, to the beginning of the text-critical enterprise, for it concerns both the goals of textual criticism and also the methods and attitudes we bring to the process. The issue of original text is very old, but one that has emerged during the past dozen years in a fresh, challenging, and perhaps disturbing fashion. In pursuing it, we will encounter very directly the interaction of traditional approaches and newly emerging postures toward New Testament text-critical theory and practice. Indeed, I would begin by asserting that textual criticism is diminished to the extent that its purpose is limited to the "quest for the original text," for we have just seen how addressing the contexts of our New Testament text and manuscripts can enlighten us and expand our horizons. Examining the very foundation of the discipline might do the same.

It will surprise no one that virtually all textual critics from the outset of the discipline have assumed that their goal is to discover

146. For full (and overlapping) discussions, see Epp, "New Testament Papyri at Oxyrhynchus in Their Social and Intellectual Context," 63–67; idem, "Codex and Literacy in Early Christianity and at Oxyrhynchus," 32–34.

147. See Epp, "New Testament Papyri at Oxyrhynchus: Their Significance."

and restore the original text of the New Testament or, taking a narrower view, to isolate the original reading at each given point of textual variation between our New Testament manuscripts. One may look at both early and current manuals of textual criticism and find typical statements, such as this one by Alexander Souter in 1913: "Textual criticism seeks, by the exercise of knowledge and trained judgment, to restore the very words of some original document which has perished."[148] Jumping ahead fifty years, J. Harold Greenlee's 1964 manual states, "Textual criticism is the study of copies of any written work of which the autograph (the original) is unknown, with the purpose of ascertaining the original text."[149] In both cases, *original* means *autograph*. A somewhat different formulation comes from Kurt Aland and Barbara Aland, who assert very directly, "Only *one* reading can be original."[150]

The obvious assumptions that underlie such statements are that a *single* original reading can be discovered and that, in a larger sense, a *single* original text can be reconstructed. And that seems self-evident, does it not? Yet, this has become an open question.

As a parallel development beginning already in the nineteenth century, many—perhaps most—textual critics used the term *original text* more cautiously, for they realized increasingly that any certainty about the text that New Testament authors wrote was more and more elusive, especially as new manuscript discoveries brought into view more and more variant readings and as increasing complexity accompanied the application of the critical canons that were supposed to facilitate the identification of the original readings. Hence, textual critics, at least since Samuel Tregelles in 1854, began to speak of their goal as the restoration or reconstruction of the New Testament text "as nearly as can be done on existing evidence."[151] Hort uses similar

148. Alexander Souter, *The Text and Canon of the New Testament* (London: Duckworth, 1913 [2d ed. in 1954]), 3.
149. J. H. Greenlee, *Introduction to New Testament Textual Criticism* (Grand Rapids: Eerdmans, 1964), 11; (rev. ed.; Peabody, Mass.: Hendrickson, 1995), 1.
150. Aland and Aland, *Text of the New Testament*, 280.
151. S. P. Tregelles, *An Account of the Printed Text of the Greek New Testament; with Remarks on Its Revision upon Critical Principles* (London: Bagster, 1854), 174. For more detail on Tregelles, see Epp, "Multivalence of the Term 'Original Text,'" 252 n. 25.

language,[152] and even B. B. Warfield expresses some reserve.[153] More recently—and more typically—Bruce Metzger's widely used handbook states that the purpose is "to ascertain from the divergent copies which form of the text should be regarded as most nearly conforming to the original."[154] Then, beginning perhaps during the last third of the twentieth century, "original text" was frequently placed within quotation marks, thereby cautioning against undue optimism.

When we ask how the term *original text* was viewed at the end of the nineteenth century, it is clear that both of the notions just reviewed were prominent, the straightforward view that textual criticism seeks to reach *the* original text of the New Testament— that is, what its authors actually wrote—but also, and more commonly, a cautious, qualified goal of recovering "the most likely original text," "the earliest attainable text," or something similar. At the outset of the twenty-first century, it is obvious that both kinds of statements are likely to remain in manuals and handbooks, but there is also the compelling conviction that matters are not quite that simple and that we need to face the complex and perhaps unsettling notion of *multivalence* in the term *original text*. In other words, the issue is more difficult, has wider implications, and is also richer and potentially more rewarding than we might have imagined.

During the past ten years or so, notably in North America and the United Kingdom, a small number of New Testament textual critics have begun to probe the phrase *original text*, have looked afresh at it, and have insisted that we ask ourselves both what we thought we meant by it and also what we now think we can mean by it. This is an issue, it should be noted at the outset, that is not for the timid or tender minded, but for those willing to

152. WH 2:1: "To present exactly the original words of the New Testament, *so far as they can now be determined from surviving documents*" (emphasis added).

153. B. B. Warfield, *An Introduction to the Textual Criticism of the New Testament* (London: Hodder & Stoughton, 1886 [7th ed. in 1907]), 15: "The autographic text of the New Testament is distinctly within the reach of criticism *in so immensely the greater part of the volume*, that we cannot despair of restoring . . . His Book, word for word, as He gave it by inspiration to men" (emphasis added to show the portion of his quotation often omitted).

154. Metzger, *Text of the New Testament*, v.

face some of the most challenging questions that the discipline
has to offer. Indeed, for some it may be a wedge that drives them
back to more traditional views and away from what is appear-
ing on the horizon. Yet, advances in knowledge seldom materi-
alize apart from bold testings of the status quo or without toler-
ation of the adventuresome spirit of the scholar willing and able
to take a risk. Not all such ventures, of course, advance knowledge and many are distinct failures, but a few do succeed and
lead us forward by directing us to their insightful though sometimes unsettling presentations.

This is not the place to rehearse fully the development of
this new understanding of original text.[155] Essentially, this
emerging stance was prompted by several observations, none
of them especially new or startling. First, for example, impetus
came from views that our present Gospels utilized preexisting
sources or existed in earlier (e.g., precanonical) forms or versions. Second, prompting came from the recognition that Acts,
for instance, has come down to us in two differing textual
streams, with the distinct probability that numerous readings
in one stream represent intentional scribal alterations (or even
reflect the possibility that the author wrote two versions of
Luke–Acts). Third, as a more specific example, these new views
were stimulated by observing that the doxology occurs after
14:23 in some manuscripts of Romans rather than in its usual
place in 16:25–27, suggesting that Romans earlier existed in a
short, fourteen-chapter version. Also of interest is the lack of *in
Rome* in Romans 1:7, 15 in a small number of witnesses, and
the similar lack of *in Ephesus* in Ephesians 1:1 in some manuscripts.[156] Data such as these (and much more could be offered) led to penetrating questions as to which is the original
Acts of the Apostles, or which is the original Romans, or Ephesians, and so on. Are the originals the texts that we have in our
canonical New Testament or some earlier, predecessor forms
that are evidenced by literary or text-critical analyses? To press
the point through another example, if it is plausible that the
Gospel of Mark used by Matthew differed from the Mark used
by Luke, then which is the original Mark? And if it is plausible

---

155. See my essay "Multivalence of the Term 'Original Text.'"
156. For details, see ibid., 262–63.

that our present Mark differed from both Matthew's Mark and Luke's Mark, then do we not have three possible originals? William L. Petersen puts it this way: "Is the 'original' Mark the Mark found in our fourth-century and later manuscripts? Or is it the Mark recovered from the so-called 'minor agreements' between Matthew and Luke? And which—if any—of the four extant endings of 'Mark' is 'original'?"[157]

Suddenly, textual criticism becomes more complex than we might wish, and similar questions arise at the level of variant readings. Here is where we may refer again to the works of Ehrman and Parker. If (à la Ehrman) textual variants reveal the alteration of a text in support, for example, of a more orthodox theological viewpoint, which text is original—the text that was altered by the scribe or the scribe's own newly altered text? If the text or manuscript in which the alteration was made becomes current in the church, as many did, do we not suddenly have two originals, one virtually lost to sight—except for the variant that was changed—and another that gained currency and recognition, eventually being accredited as canonical? The first kind of text might be called an *autographic Textform*, assuming there is no reason to think that it had itself been altered from an earlier form; and the second I designate an *interpretive Textform* because it represents an interpretation through alteration of the earlier text. If this interpretive Textform persisted until the fourfold Gospel was formed or, in the case of an epistle, until the letters of Paul were collected and more formally became canon, then the interpretive Textform is at the same time also a *canonical Textform*. I also employ the phrase *predecessor Textform* to indicate a level of text discoverable behind a New Testament writing that played a role in the latter's composition, such as the Q source, various forms of Mark, earlier forms of John or Romans, and so on. In less careful language, one might speak of an *autographic original*, a *canonical original*, or an *interpretive original*, but regardless of the terminology, there is a real sense in which every intentional, meaningful scribal alteration

---

157. W. L. Petersen, "What Text Can New Testament Textual Criticism Ultimately Reach?" in *New Testament Textual Criticism, Exegesis, and Early Church History: A Discussion of Methods* (ed. B. Aland and J. Delobel; Contributions to Biblical Exegesis and Theology 7; Kampen, Netherlands: Kok Pharos, 1994), 136–37.

to a text—whether motivated by theological, historical, stylistic, or other factors—creates a new Textform, a new original. This description of differing functions or dimensions of originality, then, is what is covered by the phrase *multivalence of the term "original" text*.[158]

And if (*à la* Parker) the Gospels and other early Christian literature circulated as a free and "living text" in the early centuries, is there an original text, or specifically a "single original text," to be recovered?[159] Parker's response, in part, is, "The question is not whether we *can* recover it, but why we want to."[160] When he asks "whether the task of textual criticism is to recover the original text," he replies, "It may be, but does not have to be,"[161] and, as we have seen, he chooses rather to emphasize the insights we gain from multiple variants. When he gets down to such cases, he concludes that, on occasion, identifying a single original reading is not possible and that, in many cases, we are instructed much more by considering the meanings of all the variants, both as they illumine the early church and as they enrich our own exegesis. And when Parker describes how variants reveal the ways in which "successive generations write on [Luke's] pages,"[162] for example, he is moving in the sphere of multiple originals or, better, of multivalence in the term *original*.

It is therefore indisputable, in my view, that the often simplistically understood term *original text* has been fragmented by the realities of how our New Testament writings were formed and transmitted, and *original* henceforth must be understood as a term designating several layers, levels, or meanings, though I prefer to call them *dimensions* of originality.

Conclusion

Since its beginnings in the Renaissance with Erasmus, during its youth throughout the Enlightenment (with Mill, Bentley,

158. For details, clarifications, and cautions, see Epp, "Multivalence of the Term 'Original Text,'" esp. 276–77.

159. Parker, *Living Text of the Gospels*, 3–4, 208.

160. Ibid., 209.

161. Ibid., 182.

162. Ibid., 174 (quoted earlier).

Bengel, Wettstein, Semler, and Griesbach), and during its young adulthood (with Lachmann, von Tischendorf, and Tregelles) and its early maturity (with Westcott and Hort and the host of scholars since then) in the nineteenth and twentieth centuries,[163] New Testament textual criticism actually has remained much the same in terms of its goals, its arguments for priority of readings, its grouping of manuscripts, and its motivation and general procedures for producing critical editions. The only sea change occurred almost precisely two-thirds of the way through this five-century period, when Lachmann's Greek New Testament of 1831 first made a clean break with the *textus receptus*, clearing the way for our prevailing critical editions, with their rather remarkable similarity ever since Tischendorf and WH. Work in these areas will go on, though skill and imagination will be required if progress is to be made.

Yet, the question of real interest, at least for me, now is this: Are we seeing the first waves (latent for a good while) of a second sea change in the new approaches described above, namely, (a) the disclosure through textual variants of scribal changes for theological reasons that have overwritten earlier readings and created new "original" readings; (b) the diminution or even the abandonment of the traditional search for the original text in favor of seeing in the living text and its multiplicity of variants the vibrant interactions in the early Christian community; and (c) the recognition that (as I wrote elsewhere) "the term 'original' has exploded into a complex and highly unmanageable multivalent entity,"[164] exposing for us various dimensions of originality in and beneath our New Testament manuscripts and readings? My answer is affirmative, but, if so, what will this "brave new world" bring, and will we be able to face the demanding but intriguing challenges that it assuredly holds?

---

163. For discussion of these various scholars and their achievements, see Epp, "Eclectic Method," 217–44 (= *STM* 144–64); idem, "Textual Criticism," 75–84 (= *STM* 17–25); "Textual Criticism (NT)," 427–30.

164. Epp, "Multivalence of the Term 'Original Text,'" 280.

2

THE CASE FOR REASONED ECLECTICISM

MICHAEL W. HOLMES

A mong the many aspects and elements of New Testament textual criticism, at the heart of the discipline are two fundamental tasks: (1) the study of the manuscripts that have preserved the text of the New Testament and (2) the evaluation of the evidence they provide. With characteristic precision Hort identified both of these (and also indicated the logical order in which they initially ought to be taken up) when he wrote, "Knowledge of documents should precede final judgement upon readings" (WH 2:31).[1] If we are to have any hope of recovering the original text of the New Testament writings, we

1. Cf. J. N. Birdsall, "The New Testament Text," in *The Cambridge History of the Bible*, vol. 1: *From the Beginnings to Jerome* (ed. P. R. Ackroyd and C. F. Evans; Cambridge: Cambridge University Press, 1970), 311.

must give full and proper attention to both of these tasks.[2] The first task involves the study of the manuscripts and other evidence (including versions and patristic citations). It focuses on the origin and history of the surviving manuscripts, the habits and characteristics of the individual scribes who copied (and sometimes corrected) them, the textual traditions to which the manuscripts bear witness, and the interrelationships between them (to the extent that they exist and can be determined). The goal of this investigation is the identification of the earliest recoverable stages of the text's transmission. Once this has, to the extent permitted by the evidence, been accomplished, it is necessary to move on to the second task. This involves the evaluation of the variant readings that represent the earliest recoverable stages of the text, with an eye to assessing, on the basis of transcriptional and intrinsic considerations, their claims to originality.[3]

To put the matter more briefly and abstractly, it is by means of external evidence that we identify the oldest surviving reading(s), which we then further evaluate by means of internal considerations.

Reasoned Eclecticism

It is the need to pay full and proper attention to both of these fundamental tasks—the study of the documents and the evaluation of the evidence they preserve—that both requires and justifies the methodological approach known as reasoned eclecticism.

2. For recent discussion of the meaning of the term "original text," see W. L. Petersen, "What Text Can New Testament Textual Criticism Ultimately Reach?" in *New Testament Textual Criticism, Exegesis, and Early Church History: A Discussion of Methods* (ed. B. Aland and J. Delobel; Contributions to Biblical Exegesis and Theology 7; Kampen, Netherlands: Kok Pharos, 1994), 136–52; M. W. Holmes, "Reasoned Eclecticism in New Testament Textual Criticism," in *TNTCR* 353–54; D. C. Parker, *The Living Text of the Gospels* (Cambridge: Cambridge University Press, 1997); E. J. Epp, "The Multivalence of the Term 'Original Text' in New Testament Textual Criticism," *Harvard Theological Review* 92 (1999): 245–81.

3. G. Zuntz, *The Text of the Epistles: A Disquisition upon the Corpus Paulinum* (Schweich Lectures 1946; London: Oxford University Press for the British Academy, 1953), 12–13; Birdsall, "New Testament Text," 316–18, 376.

By "reasoned eclecticism" I mean an approach that seeks to take into account all available evidence, both external (i.e., that provided by the manuscripts themselves) and internal (considerations having to do with the habits, mistakes, and tendencies of scribes, or the style and thought of an author).[4] Central to this approach is a fundamental guideline: the variant most likely to be original is the one that best accounts for the origin of all competing variants in terms of both external and internal evidence.[5] Reasoned eclecticism, therefore, may be differentiated on the one hand from approaches that rely primarily (if not almost exclusively) on internal criteria (usually labeled thoroughgoing or rigorous eclecticism)[6] and on the other hand from approaches that rely primarily (if not exclusively) upon external evidence (such as historical-documentary or Majority-text approaches).[7]

With respect to the history of this methodological approach known as reasoned eclecticism, a classic statement of it may be

4. See further Holmes, "Reasoned Eclecticism," 336–39; J. H. Petzer, "The History of the New Testament Text—Its Reconstruction, Significance and Use in New Testament Textual Criticism," in *New Testament Textual Criticism, Exegesis, and Early Church History: A Discussion of Methods* (ed. B. Aland and J. Delobel; Contributions to Biblical Exegesis and Theology 7; Kampen, Netherlands: Kok Pharos, 1994), 27–35; E. J. Epp, "Textual Criticism in the Exegesis of the New Testament, with an Excursus on Canon," in *Handbook to Exegesis of the New Testament* (ed. S. E. Porter; New Testament Tools and Studies 25; Leiden: Brill, 1997), 55–73, esp. 72–73.

5. Cf., e.g., Holmes, "Reasoned Eclecticism," 344–45; B. Aland, "Neutestamentliche Textkritik heute," *Verkündigung und Forschung* 21 (1976): 18; K. Aland and B. Aland, *The Text of the New Testament: An Introduction to the Critical Editions and to the Theory and Practice of Modern Textual Criticism* (trans. E. F. Rhodes; 2d ed.; Grand Rapids: Eerdmans/Leiden: Brill, 1989), 278, 280 ("only the reading which best satisfies the requirements of both external and internal criteria can be original"); G. D. Fee, *New Testament Exegesis: A Handbook for Students and Pastors* (rev. ed.; Louisville: Westminster/John Knox, 1993), 89.

6. See J. K. Elliott, "Thoroughgoing Eclecticism in New Testament Textual Criticism," in *TNTCR* 321–35; also C. Landon, *A Text-Critical Study of the Epistle of Jude* (Journal for the Study of the New Testament Supplement 135; Sheffield: Sheffield Academic Press, 1996), 13–25.

7. For the historical-documentary approach, see E. J. Epp, "Textual Criticism," in *The New Testament and Its Modern Interpreters* (ed. E. J. Epp and G. W. MacRae; Philadelphia: Fortress/Atlanta: Scholars Press, 1989), 92–94 (= *STM* 32–34); for the Majority-text approach, see D. B. Wallace, "The Majority Text Theory: History, Methods, and Critique," in *TNTCR* 297–320.

found in Westcott and Hort's famous introduction to their edition of the Greek text (WH 2:19–72). Their description and justification of the method, however, was more consistent than their practice of it, and many of the criticisms directed against WH strike more at the way they applied the method than at the method itself.[8] An updated statement that builds upon their foundation but corrects and extends their methodological superstructure is given by E. C. Colwell.[9] The most illustrative as well as methodologically sophisticated example of reasoned eclecticism is to be found in the work of Günther Zuntz.[10] His investigation of the text of the epistles begins by examining the earliest surviving documents and evidence, focusing especially on their readings; on the basis of this knowledge he then tentatively groups the manuscripts and then constructs a model of the process of transmission and corruption of the text. This history (in which, it may be noted, the Byzantine text was for Zuntz "by no means *quantité négligeable*") in turn provides a perspective from which to evaluate individual readings and establish the text.[11]

In sum, we find in Zuntz not only all the essentials of a genuinely balanced reasoned eclecticism, but also clear indications

8. See E. C. Colwell, "Genealogical Method: Its Achievements and Its Limitations," *Journal of Biblical Literature* 66 (1947): 109–33 (repr. in Colwell's *Studies in Methodology in Textual Criticism of the New Testament* [New Testament Tools and Studies 9; Leiden: Brill, 1969], 63–83); J. N. Birdsall, "The Recent History of New Testament Textual Criticism (from Westcott and Hort, 1881, to the present)," in *Aufstieg und Niedergang der römischen Welt* (ed. H. Temporini and W. Haase; Berlin: de Gruyter, 1992), 2:26:1:138–41.

9. E. C. Colwell, "Hort Redivivus: A Plea and a Program," in *Transitions in Biblical Scholarship* (ed. J. C. Rylaarsdam; Essays in Divinity 6; Chicago: University of Chicago Press, 1968), 131–55 (repr. in Colwell's *Studies in Methodology*, 148–71); see also the earlier work of M.-J. Lagrange, *Critique textuelle*, vol. 2: *La critique rationnelle* (2d ed.; Études bibliques; Paris: Gabalda, 1935), esp. 27–40.

10. Cf. the similar analysis of Birdsall ("New Testament Text," 171): "To illustrate what Colwell in his final text-critical essay was urging . . . we may take Zuntz as the prime example."

11. Note the similarity between Zuntz's approach and the five-step procedure outlined by Colwell in his final, programmatic essay ("Hort Redivivus," 160–71): (1) begin with readings, (2) characterize individual scribes and manuscripts, (3) group the manuscripts, (4) construct a historical framework, (5) evaluate readings.

as to why it is to be preferred over other contemporary approaches, such as thoroughgoing eclecticism or a purely documentary approach.

Reasoned Eclecticism vis-à-vis Thoroughgoing Eclecticism

On one level, the difference between thoroughgoing eclecticism and reasoned eclecticism may be understood as a difference in emphasis: whereas documentary evidence plays a significant role in reasoned eclecticism, thoroughgoing eclecticism
generally allows for the same evidence only a minimal role.[12] In-
dicative of this difference in emphasis, Epp characterizes those
practicing reasoned eclecticism as "eclectic generalists" (who
work with both external and internal evidence) and those pursuing thoroughgoing eclecticism as "eclectic specialists."[13] As a
consequence of this difference in emphasis, thoroughgoing
eclectics work virtually exclusively with internal criteria, having
to do with scribal habits and proclivities and authorial style and
theology.[14] Thus, for example, readings are often preferred that
are most consistent with an author's usage elsewhere in the document. In giving such decisive weight to criteria of this type,
however, thoroughgoing eclecticism gives insufficient attention
to the fundamental limitations of these criteria. For as Hort
pointed out, "it is needful to remember that authors are not always grammatical, or clear, or consistent, or felicitous; so that
not seldom an ordinary reader finds it easy to replace a feeble or
half-appropriate word or phrase by an effective substitute; and
thus the best words to express an author's meaning need not in
all cases be those which he actually employed" (WH 2:21). Thus
there is a fundamental theoretical reason why reasoned eclecti-

12. Cf. the recent programmatic statement by Landon (*Text-Critical Study*,
25), who seeks to establish the text "by relying mainly on internal evidence to
choose the best reading whenever the manuscripts divide, which places minimal reliance on external evidence."

13. E. J. Epp, "The Eclectic Method in New Testament Textual Criticism:
Solution or Symptom?" *Harvard Theological Review* 69 (1976): 211–57 (= *STM*
141–73).

14. Thus whereas reasoned eclecticism follows Hort's dictum (quoted
above) that knowledge of documents should precede evaluation of readings,
the programmatic statement by Elliott ("Thoroughgoing Eclecticism," 330)
that "knowledge of readings should precede a knowledge of MSS" stands Hort
on his head.

cism does not follow the one-sided emphasis of thoroughgoing eclecticism.[15]

On another level, the difference in emphasis between reasoned and thoroughgoing eclecticism is rooted in fundamentally different reconstructions of the history of the text, a topic to which I will return below.[16]

Reasoned Eclecticism vis-à-vis Documentary Approaches

With respect to documentary approaches, whether historical documentary or Majority text, the difference again may be understood as a matter of emphasis: whereas reasoned eclecticism attempts to work with both external and internal evidence in a balanced manner, documentary approaches place all or nearly all the weight in textual decisions on external evidence. But again (as in the case of thoroughgoing eclecticism) this difference in emphasis is rooted in a deeper issue, for the documentary approach gives insufficient attention to two fundamental limitations (one theoretical, one pragmatic) of documentary evidence for recovering the text of the New Testament.[17]

15. Thoroughgoing eclecticism is right to argue that no reading ought to be accepted or rejected merely because it does or does not occur in some favored manuscript or textual tradition. At the same time, however, the mere occurrence of a reading does not give it equal status with all other readings; when a reading occurs only in a few late witnesses, for example, it must be demonstrated, not assumed, that it could be an ancient survivor rather than a scribal correction or emendation.

16. For their views of the history of the text, see G. D. Kilpatrick, "The Transmission of the New Testament and its Reliability," in *The Principles and Practice of New Testament Textual Criticism: Collected Essays of G. D. Kilpatrick* (ed. J. K. Elliott; Bibliotheca ephemeridum theologicarum lovaniensium 96; Louvain: Louvain University Press, 1990), 3–14; Elliott, "Thoroughgoing Eclecticism," 330–31; idem, *Essays and Studies in New Testament Textual Criticism* (Estudios de Filología Neotestamentaria 3; Cordova: El Almendro, 1992), esp. 27–37; see also Petzer, "History of the New Testament Text," 30. Landon (*Text-Critical Study*, 21–22) essentially dodges the matter ("the mere fact of such lack of certainty among scholars about the early history of the text underscores the justification for a method which does not place emphasis on external evidence").

17. For an assessment of the historical-documentary approach discussed by K. W. Clark and E. J. Epp, see Holmes, "Reasoned Eclecticism," 345–49; for an evaluation of the Majority-text theory, see Wallace, "Majority Text Theory."

The theoretical limitation is this: documentary evidence can take us back to the earliest recoverable (or surviving) stage of the textual tradition, but it cannot take us any further. That is, on the basis of external evidence alone we cannot determine whether the earliest recoverable stage of the textual transmission is the autograph or a copy of it.

Consider these two hypothetical reconstructions of a simple manuscript tradition:

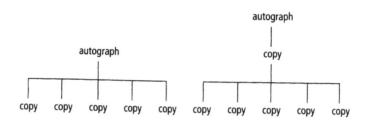

When we reach, on the basis of the surviving copies, the earliest recoverable stage of the document's transmission, have we recovered the autograph (as in the left illustration) or a *copy* of the autograph (as in the right illustration)? On the basis of documentary or manuscript evidence alone, we cannot tell. A colophon or other extratextual evidence (of which we have none from the crucial early centuries) could tell us, but the text in and of itself cannot tell us.

With respect to the New Testament, this is not a purely hypothetical situation. E. R. Richards argues that the source of the Pauline letter collection is the collection of copies of his correspondence that Paul as author would have retained—in other words, that all surviving copies of the Pauline letters derive not from the original documents, which were sent to the various churches to which they were addressed, but from a copy of the autograph that Paul had made and retained for his own use.[18]

In the case of the Gospels, we have no way of determining, solely on the basis of the manuscript evidence, whether all surviving lines of descent derive directly from the autograph or

18. E. R. Richards, *The Secretary in the Letters of Paul* (Tübingen: Mohr-Siebeck, 1991).

from a copy of the autograph (which, as a *manu*script [i.e., handwritten] copy, was an imperfect representation of the original) that the author "published"—that is, made available for others to copy.[19] At this point one may wish to make assumptions about what happened—to assume, for example, that multiple copies were made directly from the autograph and that descendants of each of these copies survived among the manuscripts known today—but on the basis of only documentary evidence this can never be more than an assumption. The fact remains that we simply don't know how many times the autograph was copied. It may have been copied multiple times, or it may have been copied only once; it may have been copied a few times, with each copy (including its mistakes) becoming the exemplar for a larger or smaller number of other copies, from which all surviving copies trace their ancestry. Whatever the actual circumstances were, they are not known, and the documentary evidence in and of itself cannot tell us.

This limitation in the very nature of external evidence is one that Colwell points out: unless external evidence takes us all the way to the autograph (in which case we would have no need of textual criticism), it cannot take us far enough.[20] Or, to quote Hort, the most that can be obtained by a purely documentary approach

> is the discovery of what is relatively original: whether the readings thus relatively original were also the readings of the autograph is another question, which can never be answered in the affirmative with absolute decision except where the autograph itself is extant. . . . Even in a case in which it were possible to shew that the extant documents can be traced back to two originals which diverged from the autograph itself without any intermediate common ancestor, we could never be quite sure that where they differed one or other must have the true reading, since they might independently introduce different changes in the same place, say owing to some obscurity in the writing of a particular word. (WH 2:66)

19. For what it meant to "publish" in antiquity, see M. W. Holmes, "Codex Bezae as a Recension of the Gospels," in *Codex Bezae: Studies from the Lunel Colloquium, June 1994* (ed. D. C. Parker and C.-B. Amphoux; New Testament Tools and Studies 22; Leiden: Brill, 1996), 142–44.

20. Colwell, "Genealogical Method," 109–33 (= Colwell's *Studies in Methodology*, 63–83).

We cannot determine, solely on the basis of external or documentary evidence, whether the earliest recoverable form of the textual tradition is the ultimate stage of the tradition (i.e., the autograph) or only the penultimate stage (a copy of the autograph from which all others copies were made). This is even more the case when, instead of a single earliest recoverable form of the tradition, we recover, as is frequently the case, *two* early forms of the tradition. Time and time again we encounter a situation where two competing readings can be traced back to the earliest discernible stage of the manuscript tradition. In such a circumstance, documentary evidence is powerless to decide between them, to tell us which is right and which is wrong (or, to indicate yet a further possibility, that neither is right). Documentary evidence can, as Zuntz observes, "throw a very considerable weight into the scales of probability," but "will not by itself suffice to determine [a] choice between competing readings."[21]

The pragmatic limitation on a documentary approach is this: every surviving manuscript, every surviving textual tradition, every surviving text-type or Textform contains errors and mistakes. To paraphrase Paul, none are perfect, not even one; all have flaws, and fall short of the glory of the autograph.

This observation is widely acknowledged.[22] It is, however, sometimes denied with regard to the Majority or Byzantine text. Thus it may be in order to offer a few illustrative instances.[23] In examples 1–3, a variant reading that arose as the result of a common scribal slip, homoeoteleuton, has become the reading of the Byzantine Textform (in the case of the first variant, the oldest witness for the Byzantine reading dates from the ninth

21. Zuntz, *Text of the Epistles*, 283.
22. Among Majority-text advocates, J. van Bruggen (*The Ancient Text of the New Testament* [trans. C. Kleijn; Winnipeg: Premier, 1976], 35) acknowledges that the Majority text as a whole preserves secondary readings.
23. The significance of these examples lies not in their number, but in that they exist at all. For the obvious genealogical significance of such nonaccidental, noncoincidental agreement in error, see (out of the many who have made the point) Robinson, "Recensional Nature," 65–67 (who affirms the point in reference to Alexandrian witnesses but rejects its application to Byzantine witnesses). See further n. 42 below.

century).[24] In examples 4–5, F. H. A. Scrivener, a contemporary critic of WH who had a much more positive view than they of the Byzantine text, rejects the Majority reading.[25]

1. 1 John 2:23: οὐδὲ τὸν πατέρα ἔχει, ὁ ὁμολογῶν τὸν υἱὸν καὶ τὸν πατέρα ἔχει
   ο ομολογων τον υιον και τον πατερα εχει ℵ A B C P Ψ 33 323 614 630 1505 1739 *al* lat sy co Or Cyp] *omit* Byz z vg^ms bo^ms RP

2. 1 John 3:1: κληθῶμεν, καὶ ἐσμέν
   και εσμεν 𝔓^74vid ℵ A B C P Ψ 33 81 614 630 945 1505 1739 1881 2495 *al* lat sy^p,h co Aug] *omit* K L 049 69 Byz vg^ms RP

3. Jude 25: ἡμῶν διὰ Ἰησοῦ Χριστοῦ τοῦ κυρίου ἡμῶν
   δια Ιησου Χριστου του κυριου ημων (𝔓^72) ℵ(*) A B C (L Ψ) 33 81 (323 630 945 1241 1739) 1505 *al* vg sy^h (co)] *omit* P Byz RP

4. John 7:8: ἐγὼ οὐκ ἀναβαίνω εἰς τὴν ἑορτὴν ταύτην
   ουκ ℵ D K 1241 *al* lat sy^s,c bo] ουπω 𝔓^66,75 B L T W Θ Ψ 070 0105 0250 f^1,13 Byz f q sy^p,h sa ac^2 pbo RP

5. 1 Peter 3:15: κύριον δὲ τὸν Χριστὸν ἁγιάσατε
   Χριστον 𝔓^72 ℵ A B C Ψ 33 614 630 945 1739 *al* latt sy co Cl] θεον P Byz RP

None of the surviving evidence, whether it be individual witnesses or specific text-types or particular Textforms, is free from blemish or flaw. This means that all surviving manuscripts, all textual traditions, all surviving Textforms preserve wrong readings.

24. See the discussion of these readings in K. Wachtel, *Der byzantinische Text der katholischen Briefe: Eine Untersuchung zur Entstehung der Koine des Neuen Testaments* (Arbeiten zur neutestamentlichen Textforschung 24; Berlin: de Gruyter, 1995), 299–300, 302–3, 376–78. In terms of raw numbers of manuscripts (of all types), support for the variants is (approximately) as follows:

Reference	Include	Omit
1 John 2:23	116	402
1 John 3:1	74	424
Jude 25	107	377

25. F. H. A. Scrivener, *A Plain Introduction to the Criticism of the New Testament* (ed. E. Miller; 4th ed.; London: Bell, 1894), 2:363, 398; see 2:321–412 for other examples. Scrivener's view of the Byzantine text was so positive that he is sometimes (but, apparently, wrongly) claimed today by Majority-text proponents as a fellow traveler; see D. B. Wallace, "Historical Revisionism and the Majority Text Theory: The Cases of F. H. A. Scrivener and Herman C. Hoskier," *New Testament Studies* 41 (1995): 280–85. Cf. Scrivener, *A Plain Introduction*, 2:274–301 (esp. 300 n. 2), where he clearly positions himself *in media res*.

For this reason alone, no single line or grouping of documentary evidence can be followed uniformly or across the board; to do so, whether as a matter of assumption[26] or mechanically[27] or on a statistical basis, is to guarantee the presence of corruption in the resulting text, because at various points all of them preserve secondary readings. In the face of such circumstances, one cannot follow any single strand of documentary evidence to the exclusion of other considerations. One must seek to utilize, in a balanced manner, all the available evidence, internal as well as external.

The Byzantine-Priority Perspective

Recently another approach has been proposed, a Byzantine-priority perspective, and it is fair to inquire where it stands in relation to reasoned eclecticism.[28] The answer to this question is not entirely clear to me. Some descriptions (which emphasize the use of both internal and external criteria) leave the impression that it is a form of reasoned eclecticism,[29] while other programmatic statements suggest it has much more in common with a documentary or Majority-text approach.[30] In the end, it may not matter: while

26. So, apparently, Robinson (e.g., "Investigating Text-Critical Dichotomy," 16); see further the discussion of the Byzantine-priority perspective below.

27. As suggested by van Bruggen, *Ancient Text of the New Testament*, 38.

28. The following published materials were available to me: the introduction in RP xiii–lvii; M. A. Robinson, "The Recensional Nature of the Alexandrian Text-Type: A Response to Selected Criticism of the Byzantine-Priority Theory," *Faith and Mission* 11 (1993): 46–74; idem, "Two Passages in Mark: A Critical Test for the Byzantine-Priority Hypothesis," *Faith and Mission* 13 (1996): 66–111; idem, "Investigating Text-Critical Dichotomy: A Critique of Modern Eclectic Praxis from a Byzantine-Priority Perspective," *Faith and Mission* 16 (1999): 16–31.

29. For example, "The Byzantine Textform can be argued *on both internal and transmissional grounds* to possess a greater claim to autograph authenticity and originality than the minority readings preferred by modern eclectic scholars" (Robinson, "Investigating Text-Critical Dichotomy," 16 [emphasis added]; cf. idem, "Recensional Nature," 49; RP xv–xvi).

30. Note, e.g., the clear emphasis on external evidence in Robinson's description of the method ("Two Passages," 67), the overall tenor of RP's introduction, and the occasional reference to "minority text readings" or "minority readings" (e.g., Robinson, "Investigating Text-Critical Dichotomy," 16). Furthermore, while the use of internal considerations is affirmed in theory, in practice they appear to play only a secondary and severely restricted role, in that conclusions reached on the basis of internal evidence are not permitted to overturn (or scarcely even to challenge) decisions reached on the basis of external arguments. They may play a decisive role in deciding between two Byzantine variants, but not in deciding between a Byzantine reading and a non-Byzantine one.

the Byzantine-priority perspective is presented as a methodological approach by means of which to recover a text, one is left, in
view of the extent to which assumptions play a foundational role,
with the impression of a text in search of methodological justification.[31] It offers a stronger critique of existing approaches than it
does an alternative to them. From a methodological perspective,
one strength is its recognition of the importance of one's view of
the history of the text for how one does textual criticism,[32] a point
to which we will return.

Summary

To summarize briefly the discussion thus far: thoroughgoing
eclecticism gives attention almost exclusively to the evaluation
of readings on the basis of internal considerations alone, to the
near exclusion of consideration of the manuscript tradition.
Documentary approaches give attention almost exclusively to
the manuscript tradition and seek to avoid the task of evaluating
readings and the use of internal considerations by choosing to
follow, to the general exclusion of other evidence, a selected
text-type or Textform. Reasoned eclecticism, aware of the limitations inherent in both approaches, seeks to take into account

31. Note, e.g., the foundational *assumption* underlying the whole perspective: "Apart from a major upheaval in the ms transmission process ('transmission history'), it is more likely that the text preserved in the majority of mss will
reflect the autograph reading than vice versa" (Robinson, "Investigating Text-
Critical Dichotomy," 16); and the claim that "a single text-type *must inevitably*
be favored as a reasonable conclusion" from a properly constructed "comprehensive transmissional history"—with no explanation or reason given for why
such an outcome is "inevitable" (Robinson, "Two Passages," 67 [emphasis add-
ed]; cf. idem, "Recensional Nature," 68 [note "of necessity"—again with no reasons indicated]). Note further the *assumption* that "theories which claim to
defend the originality . . . of minority readings are speculative at best" ("Investigating Text-Critical Dichotomy," 16), as well as the not-infrequent caricature
of alternative viewpoints or perspectives. For a particularly egregious example,
see the allegation that "modern eclecticism proceeds on the assumption that
very early in transmissional history the true (autograph) text was summarily
dissected and scattered to such remote regions of the Empire that only the enlightened scholars of modern eclecticism could possibly have the revealed in-
sight whereby to reassemble it for our own day and time" ("Recensional
Nature," 48). See also n. 43 below.
    32. E.g., Robinson, "Recensional Nature," 69; idem, "Investigating Text-
Critical Dichotomy," 29.

all the evidence in as balanced and comprehensive a manner as possible.

Both thoroughgoing and documentary approaches (and, it must be said, many examples of reasoned eclecticism as well) share a common fault: they too often attempt to make decisions about specific variants on the basis of a few overarching rules or general guidelines (e.g., adopt the reading in accord with the author's style or adopt the readings of a specific Textform). But generalizations do not necessarily apply to any specific case, and textual criticism is filled with specific cases. For we are dealing with, as A. E. Housman notes, "the frailties and aberrations of the human mind, and of its insubordinate servants, the human fingers." This means, he continues, that textual criticism

> therefore is not susceptible of hard-and-fast rules. It would be much easier if it were; and that is why people try to pretend that it is. . . . Of course you can have hard-and-fast rules if you like, but then you will have false rules, and they will lead you wrong; because their simplicity will render them inapplicable to problems which are not simple, but complicated by the play of personality. . . . A textual critic engaged upon his business is not at all like Newton investigating the motions of the planets: he is much more like a dog hunting for fleas. If a dog hunted for fleas on mathematical principles, basing his researches on statistics of area and population, he would never catch a flea except by accident. They which presents itself to the textual critic must be regarded as possibly unique.[33]

Having delineated what I understand to be reasoned eclecticism and indicated briefly how it differs from and why it is not persuaded by other approaches, let us turn to two other matters: the wide-ranging dissatisfaction with reasoned eclecticism in many quarters today and the relationship of methodology to the history of the transmission of the text.

33. A. E. Housman, "The Application of Thought to Textual Criticism," in *Selected Prose* (ed. J. Carter; Cambridge: Cambridge University Press, 1961), 132–33.

Shortcomings of Reasoned Eclecticism: Method versus Practice

If Zuntz presents a paradigmatic example of reasoned eclecticism and sets out persuasive reasons for preferring it over against its rivals, he also offers a standard against which to measure contemporary practice of reasoned eclecticism, and here we discover a major reason for much of the justifiable discontent with the method today. Too often it is utilized rather inconsistently and/or incompletely, with less than satisfactory results (including some glaring inconsistencies in textual choices). Moreover, the resulting problems and difficulties have been particularly evident because of the wide visibility of the UBS Greek text, a text produced on the basis of reasoned eclectic principles, and critics have not been hesitant to call attention to them.[34]

But the outside critics of reasoned eclecticism have not been alone in their criticism. J. Neville Birdsall, for example, a leading proponent of reasoned eclecticism, offers an incisive description of much current practice; with unsparing candor he notes that the WH edition has

> had unfortunate effects . . . Inevitably, lesser men saw in the Codex Vaticanus the "best manuscript," or derived from Hort's use of it the concept that a "best" manuscript could exist and should be followed. . . . One encountered in New Testament circles analyses of attestation of variants which ran that, such and such a manuscript in the apparatus has a "Neutral" text, and thus, it was inferred, its readings might be judged to be correct, or, alternatively, that such a witness was "Western" in type and thus not to be followed. This lack of the learning, subtlety and acumen which characterized Westcott and Hort made a mockery of their method: but their method laid itself open to such travesty. . . . Leading scholars of today were taught not to examine Hort and follow him, but to imitate wooden models such as those given.[35]

34. See especially J. K. Elliott's many (and often extensive) reviews of the UBS text, the closely associated NA[26] text, and Metzger's *TCGNT* in *Novum Testamentum* 15 (1973): 278–300; 17 (1975): 130–50; 20 (1978): 242–47; *Bible Translator* 26 (1975): 325–32; 30 (1979): 135–39; *Biblica* 60 (1979): 575–77; 62 (1981): 401–5; *Journal of Theological Studies* 32 (1981): 19–49; and elsewhere. For further bibliography, see Elliott, "Thoroughgoing Eclecticism," 333–34.

35. Birdsall, "Recent History," 141.

To turn from this broad generalization to an example of a specific problem, one unfortunate characteristic of current practice is the tendency to atomize variant readings into the smallest possible variation units and then to make decisions about each small unit in isolation from decisions about its neighbors.[36] Individual variants, however, often are part of a larger pattern or unit of variation and should not be evaluated in isolation from this larger context (which includes, in the case of the Synoptic Gospels, the parallel texts and their variants).[37]

While one could enumerate other similar concerns, let me turn instead to what may be a more significant shortcoming of the UBS text: its editors, as a group, appear to have worked without a clearly stated and jointly shared understanding of the history of the text and its transmission. The individual members of the committee certainly do have their own views about the transmission history of the text. But apparently there were within the committee significant differences of opinion on this matter, as revealed by the notes and discussion (including the many references to split opinions) in *TCGNT*, published as a companion volume to the UBS Greek text.[38]

The failure to utilize reasoned eclecticism in conjunction with at least a working hypothesis regarding the transmission of the New Testament text represents a significant shortcoming in text-critical practice. For no critical methodology (reasoned, thoroughgoing, documentary, Byzantine-priority, or whatever) works in a vacuum; it functions only in conjunction with a view of the history of the transmission of the text.[39] Zuntz describes the relationship between the two as a fruitful circle:

36. One consequence is that occasionally a text is constructed that is found in no surviving manuscript. Though this is not necessarily problematic, it can become so. For examples of the phenomenon, see Robinson, "Investigating Text-Critical Dichotomy," 17–19.

37. For examples of the evaluation of variants in their larger context, see M. W. Holmes, "The Text of Matthew 5:11," *New Testament Studies* 32 (1986): 283–86; idem, "The Text of the Matthean Divorce Passages: A Comment on the Appeal to Harmonization in Textual Decisions," *Journal of Biblical Literature* 109 (1990): 651–64.

38. The brief sketch of the history of the text in *TCGNT* 3*–7* appears to reflect primarily the view of Metzger. For the Alands' discussion, see their *Text of the New Testament*, 48–71.

39. See further on this point Holmes, "Reasoned Eclecticism," 349–53.

> Every variant whose quality and origin has . . . been estab-
> lished must serve as a stone in the mosaic picture of the his-
> tory of the tradition, for there is next to no other material
> from which it could be built up. At the same time the evalua-
> tion of individual readings depends to a large extent upon
> their place within this picture. This is another instance of that
> circle which is typical of the critical process; it is a fruitful and
> not a vicious circle.[40]

In short, the evaluation of individual readings depends greatly
on how the critic views them in relation to the larger picture
of the history of the text, because there is a synergistic relationship between history and method.

So here we have (in addition to the inconsistency and/or in-
completeness with which the method has been employed) a second reason for the confusion experienced today among those
utilizing a reasoned eclectic approach. The problem, however, is
not the method itself, but the lack of a coherent view (or even
working hypothesis) regarding the history of the transmission
of the text. The results produced by the application of any text-
critical method rest heavily upon not only the skill with which it
is exercised but also the view of the history of the text upon
which it is based.

The Transmission of the Text of the New Testament

One of the major reasons why I am not persuaded by approaches other than reasoned eclecticism involves the matter
of the history of the text. Briefly stated, I do not find persuasive the proposals regarding the history of the transmission
of the text associated with these other approaches: neither,
for example, Kilpatrick's (that virtually all variants came into
existence prior to 200 c.e., and thus [to quote Elliott] "external evidence as such is of little relevance")[41] nor Robinson's
(which is built upon assumptions, assertions, and unsubstan-
tiated claims of historical "inexorability," "inevitability," or

---

40. Zuntz, *Text of the Epistles*, 13.
41. Elliott, "Thoroughgoing Eclecticism," 331. See the perceptive analysis
by D. C. Parker in his review of Kilpatrick's *Principles and Practice of New Testament Textual Criticism*, *Journal of Theological Studies* 43 (1992): 212–13.

"necessity").[42] Instead, it is Zuntz (again) who offers a model for understanding the history of the text that makes the best sense in light of what is known about it. Despite many remaining uncertainties, there are some relatively established points upon which to build; a list of such points might include (in no particular order) the following considerations:

- Every manuscript, every textual tradition, every Textform bears within it the evidence of corruption.[43]
- The story of the text from the late first or early second to the fifth century or so is in general the story of a progression from a relatively undisciplined to a relatively more disciplined transmission of the text, with relative stability of textual traditions or Textforms being one consequence of that progression.[44]

42. E.g., RP xxix–xxxi; Robinson, "Recensional Nature," 58, 64–65, 68; idem, "Two Passages," 67; idem, "Investigating Text-Critical Dichotomy," 16. It has been observed by Colwell ("Hort Redivivus," 158–59) that Hort's goal of discrediting the Byzantine text colored his view of the history of the text; it is deeply ironic that Robinson's goal of accrediting the Byzantine text similarly appears to have colored his view of the history of the text.

43. Though Robinson does not state the following point in so many words, his published essays leave one with the clear impression that he holds (virtually as an a priori or foundational assumption) that the true reading of the text must always be found in the Byzantine textual tradition (or, to turn the point around, a variant reading with no Byzantine support cannot be original). If so, then here, ironically, is the reverse of Hort: whereas on Hort's view of the history of the text, no reading attested only by Byzantine witnesses could be genuine, seemingly on Robinson's view of the history of the text no reading attested only by non-Byzantine witnesses could be genuine. This point may in fact represent a fundamental line of demarcation between reasoned eclecticism and the Byzantine-priority approach. In the form of a question, the point is this: are there any places where (a) non-Byzantine witnesses preserve the reading of the autograph and (b) the Byzantine textual tradition does not? If the answer to this question is no, then Robinson's hypothesis regarding the transmissional history of the New Testament text is possible. If, on the other hand, the answer is yes—if, that is, there are places where non-Byzantine witnesses preserve the reading of the autograph and the Byzantine Textform fails to do so—then his historical hypothesis collapses, and something else must be considered.

44. Cf. Colwell, "Hort Redivivus," 164; and Zuntz, Text of the Epistles, 263–83. Regarding the relative lack of control during the earlier centuries, cf. (with due allowance for a bit of hyperbole) Origen's observation: "It is evident that the differences between the manuscripts have become numerous, due either to the

- In light of what is known about the literary culture of antiquity, many (perhaps most) of the nonaccidental alterations made to the text during the early centuries will have been the work of users or readers of the text.[45]
- There is little evidence of "recensional" activity (in the sense of a deliberate, thoroughgoing, and authoritative editorial revision) by scholars affecting on any widespread scale the text of the New Testament (the classical scholarly tradition, with which Christian scholars were familiar, called for the collection, marking, and discussion of variant readings, but generally not for a choice between them, especially not if it involved the elimination of material); rather changes were the result of a process of *diorthosis* ("correction").[46]
- The extent and effect of *diorthosis* could vary widely: (a) it could involve as little as correcting a copy against its exemplar; (b) it could involve the correction by a reader or scribe of (what were perceived as) copyist's mistakes without reference to the manuscript's exemplar;[47] (c) it could involve the correction of a copy by means of a different exemplar (as in, e.g., $\mathfrak{P}^{66}$), in which case it could,

---

negligence of some copyists, or to the perverse audacity of others; either not caring about the correction (διορθώσεως) of what they have copied, or in the process of correction (ἐν τῇ διορθώσει) making additions or deletions as they see fit" (*Commentary on Matthew* 15.14; Greek text reconstructed by E. Klostermann on the basis of the Latin translation in GCS 40 = *Origenes Werke* 10).

45. Holmes, "Codex Bezae," 147–50.

46. Wachtel, *Der byzantinische Text*, 159–202; Zuntz, *Text of the Epistles*, 271–72; Birdsall, "New Testament Text," 328; cf. Colwell, "Method in Establishing the Nature of Text-Types of New Testament Manuscripts," in Colwell's *Studies in Methodology in Textual Criticism of the New Testament* (New Testament Tools and Studies 9; Leiden: Brill, 1969), 49–53. For a discussion of the meaning and scope of *diorthosis* in antiquity, see Holmes, "Codex Bezae," 143–45, 149–50.

47. *Diorthosis* was an activity routinely performed by readers who wished to have a reliable copy of a manuscript, especially if reading a newly copied manuscript (in which the presence of copying errors in need of correction was taken for granted). The evidence of the papyri indicates that in performing this routine activity some readers (including some copyists, but certainly not all) often "felt themselves free to make corrections in the text, improving it by their own standards of correctness, whether grammatically, stylistically, or more substantively" (Aland and Aland, *Text of the New Testament*, 69).

in the next generation of copies made from the corrected manuscript, result in substantial alteration to the character of the textual tradition being transmitted.[48]

• The Alexandrian and Byzantine textual traditions are largely the result of selection between, rather than the creation of, variant readings.[49]

• The current ratio of support for variant readings in extant manuscripts does not necessarily reflect the ratio or level of support enjoyed by these variants at earlier stages in the transmission of the text.[50]

• The transmission of the text has been decisively shaped and influenced by external circumstances that affected the history of the church, such as persecution, the rise of Islam, and the politics of the Byzantine Empire.[51] To put the matter somewhat differently, its transmission has been, in view of the loss of manuscripts occasioned by persecution, con-

48. Indeed, if the corrections were especially thorough, it is entirely possible for a given manuscript δ, copied from γ, itself in turn a copy of α corrected according to β, to look more like β than like α, even though it is the putative grandchild of the latter.

49. Zuntz, *Text of the Epistles*, 271–72, 157–58, 55.

50. For example, according to Jerome, at Matthew 5:22 most of the ancient copies do not contain the qualification εἰκῇ ("without cause"), which is, however, found in the great majority today. Similarly, the longer ending of Mark (16:9–20), today found in one form or another in nearly all extant manuscripts, "is met with in only a few copies of the Gospel—almost all the codices of Greece being without this passage" (both examples cited by B. M. Metzger, "St. Jerome's Explicit References to Variant Readings in Manuscripts of the New Testament," in *Text and Interpretation: Studies in the New Testament Presented to Matthew Black* [ed. E. Best and R. M. Wilson; Cambridge: Cambridge University Press, 1979], 180, 182). In the tenth century, Arethas of Caesarea reports that the reading of the oldest and most accurate manuscripts in Romans 3:9 is κατέχομεν περισσόν, a variant apparently not found in any extant manuscript (Birdsall, "New Testament Text," 321). In Hebrews 2:9, the variant χωρὶς θεοῦ, which occurs in numerous early fathers both Eastern and Western (indicating that it was once quite widely known), is today found in only a few (about four) manuscripts (cf. Zuntz, *Text of the Epistles*, 34–35).

51. For brief discussions, see Birdsall, "New Testament Text," 312–13; M. W. Holmes, "The 'Majority Text Debate': New Form of an Old Issue," *Themelios* 8 (1983): 16–17. Diocletian's first edict included specific orders commanding the burning of copies of Scripture, which resulted in the loss of untold numbers of biblical manuscripts (cf. W. H. C. Frend, *Martyrdom and Persecution in the Early Church* [London: Oxford University Press, 1965/New York: New York University Press, 1967], 372–77). The only major library that appears to have escaped Dio-

quest, and warfare, anything but normal. In light of this and the previous point, the supposition that the various textual traditions "maintain[ed] a similar numerical proportion throughout all copying generations" is untenable.[52]

- More than a few later manuscripts (primarily minuscules) are direct descendants (sometimes only a generation or so removed) of (sometimes much) earlier uncial manuscripts and thus preserve evidence of earlier forms of the text and its history.

- It is possible to reconstruct with some confidence the history of specific subsections of the tradition (such as family 1 or family 13 or similar groups of closely related

---

cletian's systematic destruction—the 30,000-volume collection in Caesarea utilized by Origen, Pamphilius, Eusebius, and Jerome—was later destroyed by Muslims in 638 C.E. The Islamic conquests of the seventh century included three of the five ancient patriarchates (Alexandria, Jerusalem, and Antioch), and under Islamic rule the Christian populations of North Africa, Egypt, Palestine, Syria, and Mesopotamia either disappeared or were greatly reduced, with corresponding effects on the need for and hence transmission of Scripture in those areas.

52. Robinson, "Recensional Nature," 68; cf. idem, "Investigating Text-Critical Dichotomy," 16. An analogous example may illustrate the point. Suppose that an epidemic hits a country populated by equal numbers of four different ethnic groups. Once the epidemic has run its course and the population has regained its preepidemic levels, what will be the ratio of the four groups to one another? It is impossible to predict in advance what this ratio will be: to mention only two of many possibilities, the epidemic might touch all four groups equally, or it might, due to genetically based resistance or susceptibility to the disease, wipe out one group while leaving the others untouched. In the latter instance, the postepidemic population ratio will look nothing like the preepidemic ratio. Similarly, any number of historically contingent factors—such as which surviving manuscripts were copied and under what conditions—will have shaped the postevent ratio of manuscripts in the various textual traditions far more significantly than the preevent ratio. For example, if a surviving manuscript of one textual tradition was used by a particularly influential and well-supplied scriptorium as an exemplar for replacement Bibles, it is quite possible for the preevent ratio to change dramatically following a disruptive event such as the Diocletian persecution or the destruction of libraries due to the Islamic conquest. In any case, assumptions about what "must have happened" to the textual tradition "under normal circumstances" are worthless, because the transmission of the text occurred under conditions that were anything but normal.

manuscripts), and what we learn from these smaller sections offers useful analogies by which to understand the larger process.

- The studies of patristic texts (in, e.g., the Society of Biblical Literature's series The New Testament in the Greek Fathers) offer similarly useful snapshots of specific locations at a particular time in history.
- Within general parameters, the story of the text will vary from section to section (Gospels, Acts, Pauline corpus, Catholic letters, Revelation) and even from book to book within sections (especially in the case of the Gospels and some individual letters).

In an effort to do justice to the complex and multifaceted character of the history of the transmission of the New Testament text, Zuntz utilizes the metaphor of a river or stream. The river flowing from the autographs or archetypes early divided into two main branches, one Western and one Eastern. Readings with both Western and Eastern support, though sometimes the result of cross-contamination, generally represent readings whose origins reach deep into the "great common reservoir, the popular text of the second century" from which the two branches flowed.[53] On the Western side, the various later and loosely connected forms of the Western tradition likely represent uncontrolled provincial development of an early popular Textform. On the Eastern side, the Alexandrian textual tradition represents an early and narrow channel within the larger branch, a channel that preserved many early and genuine readings that the main branch eventually lost but that also preserved some corruptions that the main Eastern branch avoided. Out of that main Eastern branch eventually arose, as the result of a long and repeated process of *diorthosis*, the now-dominant Byzantine textual tradition.[54] While individual Byzantine readings are often ancient survivors from the second-century reservoir, the Byzantine Textform as an identifiable pattern of readings most likely began to emerge in the fourth century, continued to develop until at least

---

53. Zuntz, *Text of the Epistles*, 265.
54. Wachtel, *Der byzantinische Text*, 159–202; Colwell, "Method in Establishing the Nature of Text-types," 52.

the ninth century,[55] and achieved its current numerical domina-
tion of the Greek manuscript tradition during the course of the
twelfth to fifteenth centuries.

In visualizing this process we must keep in mind a point that
Colwell emphasizes: the early history of the New Testament manuscript tradition (and, I would add, *mutatis mutandis*, of some of the
versions) is the story of a progression from a relatively undisciplined tradition to a relatively disciplined tradition.[56] The relatively
less-disciplined stages are characterized by alteration by scribes
and readers (often careless or unintentional, sometimes deliberate); the relatively (but only relatively) more-disciplined stages are
characterized by selection and correction (*diorthosis*), whose origins likely owe something to a scholarly mind-set.[57] The time of
gradual and uneven transition from one stage to the other likely extended from the mid-second century to the late fourth or fifth century. A critical aspect of this process would have been the selection
of manuscripts to serve as exemplars for copying or *diorthosis*, in-
asmuch as the character of the manuscripts chosen will have decisively shaped the character of the textual traditions flowing from
them.[58] Here the role played by chance and circumstance, while

55. Cf. Colwell ("Method in Establishing the Nature of Text-types," 52):
"Even if—and it is too big an if—every reading found in *K* existed somewhere
in the second century, *K* did not exist in the second century. If the term 'text
type' means anything, it means the entire complex of readings in its total pattern which we refer to as 'the Alpha text-type' or 'the Byzantine text' or 'the *K*
text-type.' This did not exist as the dominant element in any manuscript in the
second century. It does exist in the ninth century and later."

56. Colwell, "Hort Redivivus," 164.

57. Zuntz (*Text of the Epistles*, 271–78) suggests that the earliest efforts
along these lines likely occurred in Alexandria, where older (and generally very
good, but not perfect) manuscripts were selected as the basis of efforts to remove and prevent corruption of the text.

58. It is precisely this unpredictable element of choice that renders uncon-
vincing Robinson's claim that the "cross-comparison and correction of mss by
reference to additional exemplars would serve to stabilize, restore, and preserve the Greek NT text *in a form which ever more steadily would approximate
the autograph text*" ("Two Passages," 108 n. 55 [emphasis added]); cf. RP xxx–
xxxi: after the "original Byzantine Textform" had "rapidly degenerated into the
various uncontrolled popular texts," it "was only natural" that widespread
cross-comparison and correction of manuscripts would result in "spontaneous
'improvement'" that would "inexorably" and "inevitably" result in the recovery
of the autograph text. There is, however, nothing inevitable or inexorable
about such a process; the outcome depends almost entirely upon the character

not recoverable in any detail, must nonetheless be granted due allowance in any attempt to describe the history of the transmission of the text. For example, an influential church leader (such
as John Chrysostom) supplies, or someone in a centrally located
and/or better-supplied scriptorium (in Constantinople, for example) chooses—perhaps for reasons having nothing to do with textual character, such as greater legibility, layout, format, or arrange-
ment of text, or simply because it was close at hand—a manuscript
as an exemplar from which to make new copies and a standard
against which to correct existing ones; and as a result the Bibles in
use in the area(s) influenced by that leader or scriptorium begin to
reflect the textual character (whatever it happens to be) of the selected model. Upon such historically contingent choices, made by
people and for reasons about which we know much less than we
would wish, turns the story of the transmission of the text of the
New Testament. As we seek to recover and reconstruct that story
on the basis of the tantalizing and incomplete evidence available to
us, we must remember that we are dealing with choices and decisions shaped by circumstance, happenstance, and the not-always-
predictable interplay of human personality and proclivities. In
such circumstances, generalizations about style or usage or assumptions about what of necessity must have happened are of little use. Instead we must always be prepared to encounter something unique, something surprising, something unpredictable—in
short, something that may turn our careful generalizations or statistical probabilities on their heads.

Conclusion

When used in conjunction with a carefully grounded theory
of the history of the text, the approach known as reasoned eclec-

---

of the manuscripts available as standards against which to make corrections or
comparisons. Furthermore, as Zuntz points out (*Text of the Epistles*, 273–74),
"the collation of any number of manuscripts of the older type [= Robinson's
'uncontrolled popular texts'] could indeed have led to the removal of their individual faults; *but the result could only have been the emergence of an average text
of that very type. It could not have led to the production of a text the very character
of which is in its freedom from errors which had infected the bulk of the earlier
tradition*" (emphasis added).

ticism will, if carefully applied to the evidence bequeathed to us, enable us to make progress toward our goals. Given that our subject matter is, to paraphrase Housman, the human mind and its disobedient subjects, the fingers, hopes for an allegedly more "objective" method are illusory.[59] To quote Zuntz once more, "There is no *règle de fer*, no divining rod to save the critic from the strain of labour and thought."[60] In such circumstances, reasoned eclecticism is our best—indeed, our only—option.

59. The claim that some methods are more objective than others—in particular, the view that decisions based on external data are somehow more objective (or at least less subjective) than those based on internal considerations—is largely illusory and misleading. With respect to both external and internal evidence, what counts as data or evidence is a theory-driven decision, and the choice of what data to follow is inescapably subjective. Cf. L. Patterson, "The Logic of Textual Criticism and the Way of Genius," in *Textual Criticism and Literary Interpretation* (ed. J. J. McGann; Chicago: University of Chicago Press, 1985), 55–91, esp. 56–60.

60. Zuntz, *Text of the Epistles*, 283.

3

THE CASE FOR THOROUGHGOING ECLECTICISM

J. K. ELLIOTT

Scholars have been fortunate in the past decade to have available some excellent new commentaries on the Greek New Testament, including recent installments in the Word Biblical Commentary, the Anchor Bible, and the International Critical Commentary. I have examined several of them, particularly to see how they resolve text-critical issues. No exegetical commentary can ignore variants in the textual tradition if the commentary is not to accept blindly the editorial decisions of the chosen Greek testament (typically the UBS/NA editions).

Several recent biblical exegetes of the highest caliber and international renown are applying themselves to the resolution of text-critical cruxes in their commentaries on the Greek New Testament. I note, for instance, that in a discussion on Acts 20:28 C. K. Barrett debates the variants τοῦ αἵματος τοῦ ἰδίου and τοῦ ἰδίου αἵματος and also the allied variants θεοῦ, κυρίου, and κυρίου καὶ (τοῦ) θεοῦ.[1] He does so assessing such criteria as which reading seems to fit Lukan authorship the best and which are apparently the more difficult readings. W. D. Davies and Dale Allison's exhaustive commentary on Matthew discusses the reading *Jesus Barabbas* at 27:16–17, bringing forward many arguments in favor of the longer reading and reasons why the name *Jesus* was omitted by later scribes. Elsewhere they discuss the nest of readings *Gadarene, Gergasene*, and others at Matthew 8:28.[2] David Aune on Revelation 18:2–3 assesses the readings associated with the verbs *fall* and *drink* found there in differing variants and reaches a decision on the reading that "makes best sense."[3] Raymond E. Brown's commentary on the Fourth Gospel discusses the longer text *who is in heaven* at John 3:13 and accepts it as the more difficult reading. And at 8:57 he looks at the significance of the meaning for the context of the variants *how can you have seen Abraham?* and *how can Abraham have seen you?* before reaching his decision.[4]

What is significant in all these discussions is that the writers of the commentaries are assessing the possibility that all of these readings are worthy of consideration as the original text. Different criteria are applied to assist them in their decision: author's language and style and theology, the maxim *difficilior lectio potior*, and the likeliest direction of change. Whether they consciously do so or not, these and many other recent commentators are accepting the principles of thoroughgoing textual criticism. Seldom do their decisions hinge on or are they decided by external evidence, the alleged weight of the manuscript attestation, or the support any of their readings have from a favored group of manuscripts. These commentaries initially take all the variants as potentially original before reaching their decision,

1. C. K. Barrett, *A Critical and Exegetical Commentary on the Acts of the Apostles* (International Critical Commentary; Edinburgh: Clark, 1998), 2:976–77.

2. W. D. Davies and D. Allison, *The Gospel according to Saint Matthew* (International Critical Commentary; Edinburgh: Clark, 1988–97), 3:584 n. 20; 2:76–77.

3. D. Aune, *Revelation 17–22* (Word Biblical Commentary 52c; Nashville: Nelson, 1998), 3:965–66.

4. R. E. Brown, *The Gospel according to John (i–xii)* (Anchor Bible Commentary 29; New York: Doubleday, 1966), 1:133, 360.

founded on principles usually based on internal criteria and intrinsic probability, the very watchwords of those of us who espouse thoroughgoing eclectic principles. I was not being deliberately selective in the examples I chose from these commentaries. Time and time again these commentaries treat the variants carefully, thoroughly, and without prejudice. The latest International Critical Commentary, that on the Pastorals by I. Howard Marshall,[5] is particularly open to the arguments of thoroughgoing eclecticism and has a special section discussing the textual variants at the opening of each subsection of these epistles.

Thoroughgoing Eclecticism Introduced

The approach to the resolution of text-critical problems with which I have been associated and which I have practiced for over thirty years has been variously dubbed rational, radical, or thoroughgoing eclecticism. *Rational eclecticism* is an attractive description, implying, I hope correctly, that the decisions are based on reasoned arguments carefully controlled and well documented. I like that description, and it is one that has the benefit of historical continuity: M.-J. Lagrange gave the second volume of his pioneering book *Critique textuelle* the title *La critique rationnelle*. *Radical eclecticism* is a less happy description, implying a revolutionary and authoritarian approach to the issues. And *thoroughgoing eclecticism* suggests a ruthlessly applied and mechanical approach to variants; if that is the impression given by the word *thoroughgoing* then that would be wrong. I do, however, tend to apply that adjective to my work, if I am ever obliged (as in this essay) to be pigeonholed into a particular named subcategory. What I mean by *thoroughgoing* is the consistent application of criteria and principles for assessing textual variants that are based *primarily* (but not, I should add, exclusively) on internal evidence. I want to emphasize the word *primarily* because those of us (those few of us) who are thoroughgoing eclectic textual critics are not blind to the documentary evidence, as some of our critics might say. We do take account of the quality

5. I. H. Marshall, *A Critical and Exegetical Commentary on the Pastoral Epistles* (International Critical Commentary; Edinburgh: Clark, 1999).

of the witnesses, as I shall demonstrate later. Thoroughgoing textual criticism does not treat documents, that is to say, manuscript witnesses, as mere carriers of variants (an accusation I have heard from detractors). But we do not begin with a predisposed view of the superiority or inferiority of any one manuscript or manuscript grouping.

A definition of the movement I defend here is that we do indeed seek to achieve a knowledge of readings over and above a knowledge of documents. We start our work from a full *apparatus criticus*—as full an apparatus as practicable—and we pay attention not only to the reading but at a later stage to the attestation as well. Where we differ from the Majority-text approach and the local-genealogical method (the old Neutral text-type in WH's nomenclature) is in the weight we give to internal and intrinsic evidence over against external support. By "external support" I mean, of course, the number, age, and geographical distribution of the manuscripts, versions, and patristic citations in favor of any of the alternatives.

I am not especially in favor of the way in which New Testament textual critics are categorized by the sorts of headings used in discussions such as found in this volume. Obviously the methods represented by the three approaches (Byzantine priority, reasoned eclecticism, and thoroughgoing eclecticism) have differences and nuances, but in practice these methodologies cannot be confined in watertight containers. In many ways the results of the three methods do not differ in all respects.

At the 1998 Hampton Court conference organized by the Scriptorium Foundation, these differences were aired by Michael Welte (representing the Münster Institute), Jakob van Bruggen, and me on a shared platform. At that conference I think we disappointed the chairman and possibly our audience by agreeing on matters of principle and praxis more than we were disagreeing over the resultant text. Those expecting a jousting match in this medieval English castle were surprised by the three representatives' amiable concluding handshakes. Consensus, or at least mutual understanding, was established. So it is not in a confrontational, imperialistic, or arrogantly proselytizing style that I address this topic.

In reality I suspect that many New Testament scholars—especially those whose interest is the exegesis of the Greek New Testament—as well as "ordinary" readers (that is, the Bible-reading public and the faithful who depend on English versions of the Scriptures) are thoroughgoing critics, as I have defined the term, without their always realizing it.

Let me explain first with reference to those readers dependent on a modern English version, be it the New Revised Standard Version, Revised English Bible, Jerusalem Bible, or New International Version. Most of these editions have footnotes indicating important textual variants, usually those of theological significance and obviously those that can be demonstrated in translation. These are normally introduced by words such as "Some ancient authorities here read . . ." or "Some manuscripts add . . ." or "Some manuscripts omit these words" and so on. The precise details of what these ancient authorities are, what the exact manuscripts are, their names, numbers, or antiquity are not shown. Readers of these notes are presumably expected to observe that the text the translators have given is not secure in the manuscript tradition and that an editorial decision has resulted in one variant being chosen as the lead text in the translation. The readers are informed that the alternative(s) are of importance or that the editors were in a dilemma over which variant reading to accept.

The choice available to the translators is exposed to the reader with the suggestion perhaps that the alternative could well be as acceptable as the canonical text of this translation as the chosen reading.[6] Whether many readers take advantage of this opportunity or invitation to accept or reject the translators' choice is questionable. I suppose most readers ignore footnotes or are prepared to accept the editors' decision as to what is printed. I suspect, however, that some of our supposed unprofessional readers, the average man or woman in the street or in the pew, may be somewhat disturbed, if they ponder the issue at all, to be shown that holy writ has not been transmitted inviolate in unchanging, carefully monitored copies presided over by scribes and ecclesiastical authorities determined to ensure conformity. Instead they see that the New

---

6. This is an aim of NA. The introduction NA[27] now states (45*–46*): "[NA[27]] intends to provide the user with a well-founded working text together with the means of verifying it or alternatively of correcting it."

Testament text, like copies of secular literature, was sometimes carelessly transcribed and that errors were introduced;
they may be even more alarmed when they see that deliberate
changes, which in many cases involve theologically sensitive
subjects, were introduced and that these may have had the effect of altering or distorting the original. It was with such readers in mind that the late Ian Moir and I decided to write a
primer explaining the significance of these text-critical notes
in the margins of modern English editions.[7] After Moir's death,
I completed the monograph, and in it I tried to show how
some of the more popular variations were likely to have arisen
and also tried to provide relatively neutral guidelines for how
one could decide among the alternatives.

In so doing, I referred to the principles on which decisions
about the text could be reached. Many of these are not dissim-
ilar to those allegedly espoused by the editors of UBS as revealed in the introduction to *TCGNT*.[8] The principles set out in
this companion volume to UBS (under "Outline of Criteria: II.
Internal Evidence") are, in most cases, those that I, as a so-
called thoroughgoing critic, also subscribe to; for instance,
"the more difficult reading is to be preferred" (A1); "scribes
would frequently bring divergent passages into harmony with
one another" (A3); scribes would sometimes "alter a less refined grammatical form . . . in accord with contemporary Atticizing preferences" (A4b); and the textual critic takes into account "the style and vocabulary of the author throughout the
book" (B1a).

The problem for the UBS committee was that these principles were appealed to only when the editors' favorite manuscripts are divided, typically when א and B support differing
readings. Thus the principles are good but are not applied
consistently; in other words, they are not used in a thoroughgoing way. The editors often felt an inability to apply their
own good rules when the manuscript tradition was deemed
"weak." Not that I accept all their principles. One principle
that exerted undue influence was A4c: scribes sometimes

---

7. Keith Elliott and I. Moir, *Manuscripts and the Text of the New Testament*
(Edinburgh: Clark, 1995).

8. *TCGNT* xxvi–xxviii (1st ed.); 12*–14* (2d ed.).

"add[ed] pronouns . . . to make a smoother text" (this principle cannot be accepted as valid, for the opposite seems to be true of certain apparently redundant pronouns or postpositional pronouns). This is one of several principles that I find myself repeatedly criticizing in various editions of the UBS and NA texts in a stream of reviews over the years.[9] In most cases, however, it is not the principle itself that is at fault but the editors' reluctance to follow their own criteria fully and consistently. I urge the application of these and other principles, and I suggest doing so without heeding the external evidence in the first instance.

Let us now turn to the use of those principles that I applied when assessing textual variants in a number of articles over the years. These concern an author's language and style; a recognition that scribes tended to assimilate parallel passages, not only within the Gospels (where this phenomenon is strongest) but elsewhere, and often where Old Testament citations are involved; an awareness of paleographical considerations like homoeoteleuton, which may be responsible for errors being made by scribes; and the theology of the first and subsequent centuries, because variants are to be seen in the context of the development of early Christianity.

Usually these eclectic principles, consistently applied, serve as useful aids in the discussion of many types of variants and enable me to reach a decision about which reading is original and which secondary. I must, however, confess to being more comfortable accepting a variant that has a fair measure of manuscript support, but I cannot refrain from drawing attention to the following UBS/NA readings that have scant manuscript support:

9. My reviews of the UBS/NA editions appear *inter alia* in *Novum Testamentum* 15 (1973): 278–300; 17 (1975): 130–50; 20 (1978): 242–47; *Bible Translator* 26 (1975): 325–32; 30 (1979): 135–39; *Biblica* 60 (1979): 575–77; 62 (1981): 401–5; *Journal of Theological Studies* 32 (1981): 19–49. Another UBS principle that I criticize is A2 ("In general the shorter reading is to be preferred"), which is also improbable. Scribes were more prone to omission than addition. Omission was a frequent occurrence—more frequent than Metzger allows: his only exception is omission facilitated by paleographical considerations, such as the recurrence of words that have letters in common. Addition demands conscious mental activity.

Reference	UBS/NA Text	Manuscript Support
Acts 4:33	τῆς ἀναστάσεως τοῦ κυρίου Ἰησοῦ	𝔓⁸ Ψ 𝔐
Acts 16:12	πρώτη[ς] μερίδος τῆς	conjecture
Hebrews 7:1	ὁ	C* 𝔐
Hebrews 12:3	ἑαυτόν	A P 104 pc
Revelation 18:3	πέπωκαν	1006ᶜ 2329

Some of the signed dissentient notes in *TCGNT* argue for the validity of a particular reading regardless of its support. For example, at Mark 10:2 (*TCGNT* 88) Bruce Metzger and Allen Wikgren (two members of the editorial committee) argue that the reading προσελθόντες (οἱ) φαρισαῖοι, accepted as original by their fellow editors, in fact is an intrusion from the Matthean parallel. There only D and it (=Itala) omit this phrase and therefore support the Markan reading defended by the American editors.

We may draw attention to other ways in which the UBS/NA text may be unbalanced or even distorted. Because of its preference for ℵ and B, we have minority readings at Mark 6:33 (καὶ προῆλθον αὐτούς with ℵ B virtually alone) and 14:52 (omit ἀπ᾿ αὐτῶν with ℵ B C only).

In numerous examples throughout the New Testament, the ubiquitous brackets in the UBS/NA text are the result of the distorting influence of these two Alexandrian manuscripts, which has caused the editors to assert the validity of a shorter ℵ B text by bracketing the words of the longer reading. See, for example, Mark 3:32; 6:23, 41; 7:4 and the accompanying notes in *TCGNT*, explaining time and time again that the addition of brackets is the conventional way the committee adopted to resolve their dilemma between the application of their quite reasonable eclectic principles and their reluctance to abandon the cult of the best manuscripts. I must make it clear that I do not wish to state that ℵ and B are faulty manuscripts—far from it; they are often right, and I accept the originality of their support for the most famous and largest omission: the last twelve verses of Mark, a reading supported virtually only by these two Greek manuscripts, but I accept their text there not because it is found in these two particular manuscripts, but because I can see good reasons why the longer ending and indeed the so-called shorter ending are non-Markan.

Twenty years ago I discussed a series of variants in Mark's Gospel, arguing in favor of readings based on thoroughgoing eclectic principles.[10] Thus I favored a reading that seemed to match the Semitic word order characteristic of our first-century author at 1:27: τί ἐστιν τοῦτο; τίς ἡ διδαχὴ ἡ καινὴ αὕτη; ὅτι κατ' ἐξουσίαν καί with C K Δ, which in addition to its Semitizing word order (article + noun + article + adjective + demonstrative) also conforms to Mark's characteristic double questions followed by ὅτι (UBS/NA print τί ἐστιν τοῦτο; διδαχὴ καινὴ κατ' ἐξουσίαν καὶ . . .). On linguistic grounds I accept θυγατρὸς αὐτῆς τῆς Ἡρῳδιάδος at 6:22 with A C Θ, a reading that seems consistent with an example of Mark's preference for parentheses; here τῆς Ἡρῳδιάδος is in effect parenthetical (explaining the pronoun αὐτῆς).[11] Likewise I read αὐτοῦ after μαθηταῖς at 6:41 as characteristic not only of Markan usage but of New Testament usage as a whole. Also I argue for ὃς οὐκ ἀκολουθεῖ ἡμῖν at 9:38 with A K Π, a repetition not uncharacteristic of Mark. It will be seen that when dealing with author's style (in particular) I attempt to establish firm uses and then to sort out nonconforming examples with the aid of the apparatus to produce a general statement of the usage.

Elsewhere I have put forward the case for thoroughgoing eclecticism as a methodology, establishing the rules and principles that demonstrate that thoroughgoing eclecticism is not a subjective exercise.[12] In the remainder of this essay, I wish to

10. J. K. Elliott, "An Eclectic Textual Commentary on the Greek Text of Mark's Gospel," in *New Testament Textual Criticism: Its Significance for Exegesis: Essays in Honour of Bruce M. Metzger* (ed. E. J. Epp and G. D. Fee; Oxford: Clarendon, 1981), 47–60.

11. See C. H. Turner, "Notes on Markan Usage," *Journal of Theological Studies* 26 (1924–25): 235–37 (repr. in *The Language and Style of the Gospel of Mark* [ed. J. K. Elliott; Novum Testamentum Supplement 71; Leiden: Brill, 1993], 47–48).

12. Most recently in "Thoroughgoing Eclecticism in New Testament Textual Criticism," in *TNTCR* 321–35.

demonstrate how these principles may be applied in a consistent way by examining a typical set of examples such as would be encountered when tackling variants during an exegetical study of the New Testament text.

Thoroughgoing Eclecticism Illustrated

Mark 1:4

The UBS text confuses readers by its use of brackets: [ὁ] βαπτίζων ἐν τῇ ἐρήμῳ. Many students are unsure whether to omit the bracketed word or to ignore the brackets. In this verse, if they do the former, then they understand the subject to be Ἰωάννης *solus* and the verb ἐγένετο either as a kind of periphrastic ("John was baptizing and preaching") or with the sense "John came, baptizing and preaching." If, however, readers ignore the brackets, they accept the presence of the article (and omit καί), which has the effect of taking ὁ βαπτίζων in apposition to Ἰωάννης. The meaning then is: "John the Baptist [lit., the baptizing man] was preaching in the wilderness." The way the editors of UBS/NA try to resolve the differences in the variants is by appealing to the readings in their favorite manuscripts. But as ℵ and B support different readings here, our editors were in a quandary—hence the use of brackets to conceal a dilemma among members of the committee.

Others may choose to follow the reading of the Majority text, which has βαπτίζων ἐν τῇ ἐρήμῳ καί. Thoroughgoing eclecticism seeks to broaden the inquiry by asking questions such as: What does Markan usage teach us here? The main line of inquiry is then to investigate Mark's way of describing John elsewhere. What we learn from this is that each of the other four places where John appears (6:14, 24, 25; 8:28) also exhibits textual variation between the participle βαπτίζων and the noun βαπτιστής. Later Christian writers (from Matthew and Luke onward) use βαπτιστής as the preferred name to describe John—it was a noun coined by Christians especially for this purpose. But in Mark the verbal form is likely to have been current in the primitive church, and it was this participle that was later altered to forms of the newfangled noun by scribes. I therefore argue in favor of forms of βαπτίζων at 6:14, 24, 25;

8:28.[13] The UBS agrees with that judgment at 6:14 and 6:24 only, thus giving Mark an implausibly inconsistent pattern of usage, although there are variants giving forms of βαπτιστής in all four verses. Thoroughgoing eclecticism accepts the probability of Markan consistency in these matters. At 6:25 βαπτίζοντος is read with only L 700 892, and at 8:28 βαπτίζοντα is read with only 28 and 565.

Detractors may wish to make the point that an author like Mark cannot be expected to have written in a wooden, mechanical way and therefore may not have been consistent in this matter. May it not be, they argue, that Mark was composing his Gospel at a time when Christian usage was on the change, that the newfangled βαπτιστής *was* known but not fully established in common speech, thus his oscillating reflects precisely the changing Christian vocabulary?

My own impression is that, despite the relative paucity of manuscript support for forms of βαπτίζων at 6:25 and 8:28, Mark in fact used only βαπτίζων and that we have five occurrences, four of which have variant βαπτιστής and the other (at 1:4) that was not recognized by all witnesses as a substantive.

This would then help in the elucidation of the variants at 1:4. It is not surprising that on his first introduction John would be described fully, and not merely as "John." So Ἰωάννης ὁ βαπτίζων here is Mark's way of describing the distinctiveness of this figure.

Mark 10:1

Another variant that I regularly use as an example of how the variants enable us to recognize (and restore) Markan consistency is at 10:1. Mark uses ὄχλος some forty times in the Gospel. These are firmly established. Only at 10:1 do modern printed editions give the plural συμπορεύονται . . . ὄχλοι, but the variant συνέρχεται . . . ὁ ὄχλος read by D Θ *al* is likely to be original.

I am not convinced by the argument that scribes imposed conformity on Mark by writing the singular; unlike us, scribes would not have been able to see at a glimpse in a concordance that Mark overwhelmingly used the singular. Mark obviously

13. J. K. Elliott, "*Ho Baptizōn* and Mark i 4," *Theologische Zeitschrift* 31 (1975): 14–15.

would have known the plural form of ὄχλος but perhaps chose never to use it because for him the singular meant "a great number of people," and the plural "crowds" would not have contained anything different in meaning for him. Thoroughgoing eclecticism explains the change from the original singular to have been motivated by the common scribal tendency to harmonize parallel passages. Here Matthew 19:1 reads ὄχλοι. Unlike Mark, Matthew uses both singular and plural ὄχλος throughout his Gospel.

Acts 7:56

An intriguing variant occurs at Acts 7:56: ἀνθρώπου versus θεοῦ. G. D. Kilpatrick considered θεοῦ (read by 𝔓⁷⁴ 491 614 bo [two manuscripts] Geo) to be the original reading.[14] On the grounds of thoroughgoing eclecticism this proposal has much merit. According to him, stylistically conscious scribes would have had good reason to reduce the number of occurrences of θεός in this passage, but by altering θεοῦ to ἀνθρώπου they created the only occurrence of the title *Son of Man* outside the Gospels. Obviously the title was well known to early Christians and to scribes, but there are no theological reasons why Luke would have wanted Stephen to have been the only character apart from Jesus to have spoken of the Son of Man, especially as the *standing* Son is different from the usage in the Gospels.

Hebrews 2:9

Nearly thirty years ago I examined the intriguing variation unit at Hebrews 2:9, where the manuscripts read either χάριτι θεοῦ or χωρὶς θεοῦ.[15] I argued then in favor of χωρίς. Ehrman too accepts the internal criteria as decisive, while drawing our attention to the fact that, although we have very few witnesses favoring the reading χωρὶς θεοῦ, nonetheless Origen in his day

14. G. D. Kilpatrick, "Acts vii 56: Son of Man?" *Theologische Zeitschrift* 21 (1965): 209; idem, "Again Acts vii 56: Son of Man?" *Theologische Zeitschrift* 34 (1978): 232 (both repr. in *The Principles and Practice of New Testament Textual Criticism: Collected Essays of G. D. Kilpatrick* [ed. J. K. Elliott; Bibliotheca ephemeridum theologicarum lovaniensium 96; Louvain: Louvain University Press, 1990], 415–18).
15. J. K. Elliott, "When Jesus Was Apart from God," *Expository Times* 83 (1972): 339–41.

claimed that this was a popular reading known in many manuscripts.[16] Χωρὶς θεοῦ is the more difficult of the two readings. It seems to fit with the early first-century belief that at the point of his death the incarnate Jesus was by definition separated from God; it is a belief echoed in the Old Testament (where the hope is sometimes expressed that at a point in the future God would stretch out his hand into Sheol to awaken the sleeping spirits) and is found in Matthew's and Mark's accounts of the death of Jesus, which have him cry from the cross that God is about to abandon him. Jesus' cry of dereliction on the cross is part of a theology that sees in death—even the death (especially the death) of the one who was to be raised from death three days later—a state "without God." Controversies in the fifth century concerned with the divine nature of Christ meant that χωρὶς θεοῦ could be construed in some circles at that time to imply that Jesus' divine nature had not shared in his suffering: that was a function only of his human nature. Among the witnesses for χωρίς are some Syriac manuscripts, influenced by the teachings of Nestorius, to whom such views were attributed.

Discussions along these lines take us far beyond merely documentary concerns about accepting and printing a supposed original text based on particular manuscript support and take us away from paleographical considerations about whether careless scribes may have misread an original χάριτι as χωρίς or vice versa.

Virgin Birth

Another Christian doctrine that gained importance after the time of the composition of the New Testament books is the virgin-birth tradition.[17] Scribes of later centuries copying New Testament passages that seem not to support that tradition or that at least cast doubt on it would be tempted to make changes. We thus find textual variation in passages in which Joseph and Mary are described as Jesus' parents or in which

16. B. D. Ehrman, *The Orthodox Corruption of Scripture* (New York: Oxford University Press, 1993), 146–50.

17. Further developments of this tradition are to be seen in the noncanonical Christian literature that began to emerge from the second century onward. See J. K. Elliott, *The Apocryphal New Testament* (Oxford: Clarendon, 1993).

Joseph is described as Jesus' father. The rule of thumb to which I suspect most scholars would agree is that the manuscripts that refer to Joseph as Jesus' father are original and that changes to remove that relationship are secondary and were due to scribal attempts to protect the burgeoning beliefs in the virginal birth. Acceptance of these arguments would encourage the originality of the reading τοῦ τέκτονος υἱὸς καί at Mark 6:3; ὁ πατὴρ αὐτοῦ at Luke 2:33; and οἱ γονεῖς αὐτοῦ at Luke 2:41 and 2:43. Thoroughgoing critics leave it at that; others may balk at accepting a reading at Mark 6:3 with the support primarily of f^{13} 33 700 *pc.*

Matthew 21:28–32

Mention earlier of the maxim *difficilior lectio potior* brings me now to the parable of the two boys in Matthew 21:28–32. The parable is transmitted in the manuscripts in at least three main forms. In ℵ one child first refused but later changed his mind. The second child then agreed to the man's request but reneged on the promise. The child who is said to have done the father's will is identified as ὁ πρῶτος. In the reading of B the first child is the one who promises to work in the vineyard but disobeys; the second child refuses but later obeys. The child doing the will of the father is identified as ὁ ὕστερος, ὁ δεύτερος, or ὁ ἔσχατος. A third version is in Codex Bezae, which agrees with the sequence found in ℵ; but in D the child who does the will of the father is said to be the one who agrees with the request but then fails to fulfill it. Metzger's *TCGNT* (45) posits that the meaning in D is "nonsensical" and therefore to be rejected. It is not just *difficilior* but *difficilima.* Westcott and Hort took the reading in D seriously in their "Notes on Select Readings" and tried to make sense of it. Without accepting it as the original, they took the reading in D to be halfway between B and ℵ and the reason for the reading in ℵ. Jerome too tried to make sense of the reading we know from D. Recently, Michaels also tried to explain the origin of the text in D.[18]

I cannot pretend to have reached a final decision on the original form of this problematic parable. It is a crux that the Alands

---

18. J. R. Michaels, "The Parable of the Regretful Son," *Harvard Theological Review* 61 (1968): 15–26.

label one of the most difficult in textual criticism,[19] but discussions along the lines of WH, Michaels, and others (including Amphoux)[20] try to make sense of the changes and a developing tradition understood within the particular context of Matthew's Gospel and his positioning of this parable. The discussion may have been called for because B and ℵ are on different sides, but the ways in which the discussions are conducted and the ways in which scholars attempt to explain the ostensibly bizarre reading of D owe much to or at least are compatible with the principles and practices of thoroughgoing eclecticism. Again we find that thoroughgoing criticism is in the mainstream of text-critical analyses.

Luke 9:54–56

The three longer readings that occur in Luke 9:54–56 are complex, and the variants need not be set out here. Commentaries are somewhat hesitant about the status of these "additional" words. Suffice it to say that the longer readings in each of these three verses, with varying degrees of manuscript support, suggest that the three ought not to be treated together. As in the parable of the two boys, one needs to be alert to the wider context and aware that only the application of principles based on intrinsic probability (that is, a consistent application of thoroughgoing eclecticism) will resolve the textual problems in these verses satisfactorily. Holding resolutely to the Majority text or to the readings of the so-called best manuscripts will not solve the textual problems and will further serve only to camouflage the alternatives.

Western Noninterpolations

The famous but oddly named Western noninterpolations have occasioned much debate ever since WH dubbed certain shorter readings (mainly at the end of Luke's Gospel) in D and

19. K. Aland and B. Aland, *The Text of the New Testament: An Introduction to the Critical Editions and to the Theory and Practice of Modern Textual Criticism* (trans. E. F. Rhodes; 2d ed.; Grand Rapids: Eerdmans; Leiden: Brill, 1989), 312–16.

20. C.-B. Amphoux, "La transmission des Evangiles," *Le monde de la Bible* 47 (Jan.–Feb. 1987): 30–47, esp. 46–47.

its allies in this way and decided to accept their originality because they went against the normal tendency of D to support
longer readings. The debate even affects the judgments in suc-
ceeding editions of UBS, where the ratings A, B, C, and D fluctu-
ate over these variants. The confidence of its editors as revealed
by these bizarre assessments shows that, although the editors
continue to go against WH in all eight variants in Luke, the rat-
ing letters go up from D (C in the case of 22:19b–20) in UBS[1] to
B in UBS[4], even though no additional manuscript witnesses of
substance are adduced for any of the readings. The problems
met by the original committee are maintained even in the second edition of *TCGNT,* where we read in most of the entries con-
cerning these Western noninterpolations that a minority of the
five committee members dissented. If principles associated with
thoroughgoing criticism were given full sway, then each of these
passages would be treated separately and we should not be mes-
merized by WH's blanket treatment of these nine variants (and
only nine variation units amid many others) where Western witnesses support a shorter text. The debate could be more fruitful
and less divisive if each variant were treated on its own merits.
For instance, the presence or absence of a reference to Jesus' as-
cension in Luke 24:51 should be decided on the theology of
Luke in an open-minded way and not be associated with other
variants in the chapter.

Luke 22:43–44

A similarly open approach should accompany the discussion
of the variant at Luke 22:43–44, which also concerns a choice
between a longer and a shorter text. Luke's language and style
need to be considered to ascertain if these verses could have
come—or definitely could not have come—from his pen.[21] Then
one needs to take into account the possibility that assimilation
to the parallels may have played a part: the other Gospels' accounts of the Gethsemane incident have nothing comparable to

---

21. This consideration should be done in the same way as one investigates
the additions at the end of Mark or the doxology in Romans; cf. J. K. Elliott,
"The Text and Language of the Endings of Mark's Gospel," *Theologische
Zeitschrift* 27 (1971): 255–61; idem, "The Language and Style of the Concluding
Doxology to the Epistle to the Romans," *Zeitschrift für die neutestamentliche
Wissenschaft* 72 (1981): 124–30.

Luke 22:43–44, and one ought to consider if the omission of these verses from Luke was prompted by the common desire to harmonize parallels in the Synoptic Gospels. Theological considerations need to be taken into account about whether the contents of these verses, if original, would make the words liable to excision or whether they would have been added to the original composition in order to make a particular christological point. These considerations, rather than the support of manuscripts on both sides, should be the foci of prime importance. When we observe the precise manuscript attestation on both sides, we note that $\mathfrak{P}^{75}$ ℵ¹ B oppose ℵ* ℵ² D 𝔐 and that therefore these words were controversial even at an early date and that they occasioned changes in both directions in one particular manuscript.

Romans 5:1

Romans 5:1 likewise merits discussion within a theological context, that of Pauline theology as a whole. Does the fact of having been justified automatically carry with it the understanding that peace has already come about, or is the state of having been justified something that occasions the exhortation that peace should be striven for? Answers to these questions should precede discussion about whether scribes would have accidentally altered the text by writing O as Ω or vice versa. That individual manuscripts display the omicron/omega change, with correctors of both ℵ and B significantly adjusting the text here, demonstrates that deliberate change was the cause for this variant. Even the UBS committee, whose deliberations are revealed in Metzger's *TCGNT* (452), agreed (on this rare occasion!) with the majority who "judged that internal evidence must here take precedence."

1 Corinthians 13:3

Another variant in the Pauline corpus often too easily dismissed as merely orthographic is καυθήσομαι or καυθήσωμαι or καυχήσωμαι at 1 Corinthians 13:3. The discussion ought to concentrate on the situation in the career of Paul (i.e., scribes may have decided that, as Paul was not burned, this extravagant exaggeration should be removed from his epistle) rather than on which letters would have been accidentally written for another. I argue elsewhere that καυθήσομαι is probably the original text;[22] others disagree with me, but the discussion should continue with reference to the exegesis of the passage and not be based on the manuscript support for one or other of the alternatives.

Jerusalem

The name *Jerusalem*, particularly in Acts, appears in our printed editions apparently indiscriminately as either Ἱερο-σόλυμα or Ἱερουσαλήμ. I attempted to bring some order into the chaotic picture by taking advantage of the many textual variants that affect this name.[23] As a result I accept Ἱερουσαλήμ when the context is Jewish or addressed to Jews, and Ἱεροσό-λυμα in a Hellenistic context. For example, I argue for Ἱεροσό-λυμα at Acts 25:3 and for Ἱερουσαλήμ at 21:4. Some disagree with my decisions and make differing suggestions. But the debate is usually conducted using principles of usage and exegesis; seldom do the manuscript witnesses affect the judgments.

Colossians 4:15

Is the householder of the Christian meeting place in Colossians 4:15 male or female? Do we read Νυμφᾶν . . . αὐτοῦ or Νύμ-φαν . . . αὐτῆς? What was the role of women in the early church? Which reading is original? Why was it changed? Answers to these questions are needed and ought not be circumvented by a concentration on only manuscript support.

Romans 16:7

In a context similar to the above, I note the variant at Romans 16:7. This variant has received much publicity because modern attempts to create equality in the ecclesiastical workplace depend on this disputed biblical reference. Because the two main variants concern accenting, a feature not consistently applied in early manuscripts, the resolution of the issue de-

22. J. K. Elliott, "In Favour of καυθήσομαι at 1 Cor 3:3," *Zeitschrift für die neutestamentliche Wissenschaft* 62 (1971): 287–88.
23. J. K. Elliott, "Jerusalem in Acts and the Gospels," *New Testament Studies* 23 (1977): 462–69.

pends on arguments of internal considerations, the social structure of early Christianity, and church history—in other words
on the stocks-in-trade of thoroughgoing eclecticism.

1 Corinthians 15:51

Theological and exegetical motives are likely to be behind the
changes in 1 Corinthians 15:51:

a. οὐ κοιμηθησόμεθα, πάντες δὲ ἀλλαγησόμεθα
b. οὐ κοιμηθησόμεθα, οὐ πάντες δὲ ἀλλαγησόμεθα
c. ἀναστησόμεθα, οὐ πάντες δὲ ἀλλαγησόμεθα
d. κοιμηθησόμεθα, οὐ πάντες δὲ ἀλλαγησόμεθα

Thoroughgoing eclecticism seeks to explain the variations by
examining Paul's teaching on the afterlife and tries to see what
changes later generations of Christians could have made to the
original Pauline teaching, especially at a time when belief in
an imminent parousia had receded or when ideas about universal salvation fluctuated. Discussions at that level are to be
encouraged. We should not allow the discussions to be skewed
by a premature examination of the external support. As it happens, reading a is supported by B D² 𝔐, reading b by 𝔓⁴⁶ Aᶜ,
reading c by D* lat, and reading d by ℵ C.

Thoroughgoing Eclecticism and the History of the Text

This concludes my all-too-brief survey. To be thoroughgoing,
to use the *leitmotif* of this essay, one could go through all the
variation units discussed in *TCGNT* and engage with all of
Metzger's discussions from the perspective of thoroughgoing
eclectic criticism. Or one could—indeed should—examine all
the variants in the apparatus of a critical edition of the Greek
New Testament. It is, of course, an enormous task. Perhaps that
is why it is easier, safer, and less demanding if one prefers quick
fixes such as seem to be promised by an appeal to the Majority
text or to the cult of the best manuscripts.

Some critics of thoroughgoing criticism, noting quite properly its predilection for establishing rules of style and usage by

concentrating on firm examples and accepting variant readings
that conform to those patterns in places where the text is uncer-
tain, react in one of at least two ways: either by asking (a) how
certain we may be that the allegedly firm examples really are
found in all known witnesses, the question asked being whether
newly collated manuscripts may render a former certain reading insecure; or (b) whether a passage whose text is firm but
that seems to be an exception to the established norm should be
emended to make it fit the rule. The answer to the first question
seems to be that very few new manuscripts introduce genuine
new readings. They merely give additional support for readings
already logged.[24] Our stock of variation units already built up
seems to be remarkably consistent. The second question tempts
thoroughgoing criticism to be even more radical by making ab-
errant passages conform by altering the text oneself.

But thoroughgoing eclecticism sees no need to resort to conjectural emendation, which often turns out to be a mere imagi-
native rewriting of the New Testament. Conjectural emendation
of the New Testament was practiced in earlier periods, but few
of these conjectures or guesses met with widespread scholarly
acceptance. A decreasing number of some famous conjectures
are still allowed to clutter unnecessarily the apparatus of the NA
editions. Passages of great difficulty such as τὸ μὴ ὑπὲρ ἃ γέγρα-
πται at 1 Corinthians 4:6 may have to be accepted as primitive
corruptions or obscure writing by the original author. (How often are our own written words always crystal clear?) Suggested
emendations, some highly ingenious, are often improbable
merely because of their ingenuity. At Mark 10:1 we were able to
restore ὄχλος and thus have a text that conformed to Mark's established usage elsewhere. There, of course, we had manuscript
evidence available. We now ask the hypothetical question: What
if every single manuscript known to us read ὄχλοι? Would we
have emended 10:1 to read ὄχλος merely because our rule told
us what to expect? I answer no. If that had indeed been the case
we would have had to justify and explain Mark's apparently

24. Many of the latest published New Testament fragments from Oxyrhynchus add support to existing readings. There are very few unique readings;
some of those that seem to exist, often insecurely read in fragmentary manuscripts, are open to second opinions.

maverick use of the plural here by saying, as, of course, commentaries on the critical text do, that here and here only does Mark want to show that different and separate crowds descended on Jesus. Then one would say that Matthew, if he were working on Mark, took over that Markan plural in his retelling of this passage. All of that makes sense. One would not need to emend the text to achieve an acceptable meaning. But Mark 10:1 does have a textual variant that needs discussion, and it is one that I hope I explained quite convincingly. Where a unique feature occurs firmly established in the manuscript tradition, one that does not conform to the author's normal usage elsewhere, then I suggest we merely mark that passage as an exception or as a difficulty and accept it as such. We should not expunge exceptions by means of emendations.

Meanwhile, another criticism against the principles and praxis of thoroughgoing eclecticism that I should address is that we are not alert to the history of the text, by which is commonly meant that, by accepting a reading here with a few early papyri, a reading there with a few Byzantine witnesses, and another reading elsewhere supported by Western manuscripts, we are blithely oblivious to any kind of continuum.[25] Just because we do not subscribe to the supremacy of, say, the Alexandrian witnesses or are skeptical about the automatic originality of the Majority text-type does not mean that we ignore the changes and historical developments of the New Testament text.

Thoroughgoing eclecticism has high respect for the history of Christian doctrine, as I hope I demonstrated in some of the examples set out here and in other of my writings. The interests of the church and ecclesiastical controversy are regularly taken into account in assessing the likeliest direction of change in certain types of textual variation. We also attempt not only to reach a decision about which reading is more likely to represent the original words of the original author but the motive for the change(s) found in the alternative reading(s). Thoroughgoing eclecticism, with its stated aim of trying to do more than merely

25. See, e.g., G. D. Fee, "Rigorous or Reasoned Eclecticism—Which?" in *Studies in New Testament Language and Text: Essays in Honour of George D. Kilpatrick on the Occasion of His Sixty-Fifth Birthday* (ed. J. K. Elliott; Novum Testamentum Supplement 44; Leiden: Brill, 1976), 179–97 (= *STM* 124–40).

establish a critical text, copes well with these historical questions. One can trace early ecclesiastical controversies in the *apparatus criticus* to a Greek New Testament.

The same is true when we turn to the history of the Greek language. Thoroughgoing eclecticism uses the changes introduced under the influence of Atticism, especially. Again, the *apparatus criticus* reveals many variants that seem to have come about as a result of the stylists' criteria. Educated scribes were influenced by the neo-Atticist grammarians from the second century onward.[26] Thoroughgoing eclecticism, by isolating variants that ring true of first-century Semitized Hellenistic Greek features found in the text, draws attention to readings that conform to the language likely to belong to that of the original authors, especially when the alternatives agree with norms compatible with (and, ideally, actually commented on by) the Atticist grammarians, copies of whose writings have come down to us. This exercise too pays due regard to historical developments. What thoroughgoing eclecticism is unable to do is to pronounce that the paleographical dating and geographical provenance of any manuscript are relevant in enabling us to pass judgment on the worth of the readings within it.

Near the beginning of this essay I stated that thoroughgoing eclecticism is not blind to the character of documentary evidence. Knowledge of readings must precede knowledge of documents. But even for thoroughgoing eclectic critics, documents are no mere carriers of variants. We do—and should—observe the characteristics of manuscripts. If, for instance, a witness regularly expands divine titles, possibly using established liturgical formulas, then we will be reluctant to accept its testimony as a reliable witness to the original text in this matter in a variation unit. Likewise a manuscript that seems to be regularly feck-

26. I discuss the influence of grammarians Phrynichus and Moeris in (among other places) "Phrynichus' Influence on the Textual Tradition of the New Testament," *Zeitschrift für die neutestamentliche Wissenschaft* 63 (1972): 133–38; and "Moeris and the Textual Tradition of the Greek New Testament," in *Studies in New Testament Language and Text* (ed. J. K. Elliott; Novum Testamentum Supplement 44; Leiden: Brill, 1976), 144–52 (both repr. under the title "The Atticist Grammarians," in my *Essays and Studies in New Testament Textual Criticism* [Estudios de Filología Neotestamentaria 3; Cordova: El Almendro, 1992], 65–77).

less in matters of word order would tend to rule its witness out of court when assessing variants of this sort.

I recently examined a sequence of variants in Acts and noted that a strict application of thoroughgoing eclectic principles enabled me to explain how most of the variants arose and where the original text—or at least the *Ausgangstext*—was. I observed the ways in which the manuscripts related to my chosen original readings and saw that one or two witnesses were frequently in the wrong camp. I cannot explain why these manuscripts should be such poor supporters of my proposed original text in Acts, but that kind of observation meant that I am chary about accepting as original or really further considering readings supported exclusively by those manuscripts. To admit this may imply that I am abandoning a theory that is prepared to accept an original reading no matter where it is found and occasionally even to print as original a reading found in only one witness. But what I am conceding is that by examining without prejudice the readings in all manuscripts we may at a later stage reach decisions about the relative worthiness of particular witnesses to support, perhaps even singly, the original text. To be really thorough I suggest that we do our textual criticism eclectically without bowing to preconceived theories about the alleged superiority of certain witnesses. Then, having done our work, I suggest that we review the behavior of individual witnesses—in effect, rate them. Those that fall below a certain level of accuracy would in the future be regarded with some suspicion. Thoroughgoing eclecticism may in fact be a better way of ultimately enabling scholars to make certain deductions about the reliability (or nonreliability) of witnesses. If so, thoroughgoing eclecticism is not then ignoring the value of manuscripts. But even if this may be carried out in any meaningful way—and it is clearly one that demands an enormous amount of labor—I cannot claim that that is an overriding interest or concern of thoroughgoing eclecticism. The main purpose is to enable the history of the text itself to be plotted—and that is a task of truly historical significance.

Thoroughgoing eclecticism is very much alert to the development of Christian doctrine and the awareness that this sometimes caused changes in the manuscript tradition. Bart Ehrman has put us very much in his debt with his *Orthodox Corruption of Scripture* by showing how various pressure groups in early Christianity left their fingerprints on manuscripts because their deliberate changes to the text, especially those relating to important issues of Christology and theology, caused changes to the text being transmitted in one direction or another in support of a particular party line. His reasoning can be harnessed when assessing textual variants; often his work is compatible with the aims and practices of thoroughgoing eclecticism.

Conclusion

I have tried to indicate in this essay that, on the level of theory and principle, thoroughgoing eclecticism is not widely divergent in its views compared with the approaches adopted by other eclectic scholars. The difference is detected in the application of these principles when assessing textual variants. As we see, the UBS editors occasionally bravely print readings not necessarily always supported by their usual crop of witnesses, but generally they abandon arguments based on their published principles if the manuscript support is deemed to be inappropriate.

Thoroughgoing textual criticism should be concerned not only with establishing as far as possible the original words of the original authors; it should try to explain the likeliest direction of change and why the secondary texts arose. It may well be that modern textual criticism is less confident about the need to, or its ability to, establish the original text and that its best contribution to biblical studies is to show how variation arose, ideally in what directions, and to explain the significance of all variants. This latter concern is especially important at a time when scholars are increasingly aware that each and every manuscript of the Greek New Testament was the canonical Scripture used and lived by its owners—even maverick or secondary readings as judged by modern scholarship were the biblical texts of those believers. To jettison secondary readings as mere aberrations without seeking to understand their meaning, the reason for their existence, or their influence is to abandon a fruitful source of knowledge about the development, history, and use of these living words no matter where they happen to be located.

4

THE CASE
FOR BYZANTINE
PRIORITY

MAURICE A. ROBINSON

> There has been no change in people's opinions of the Byzantine text. Critics may be kinder to Byzantine readings—but for reasons not related to their Byzantine nature. It's not really much of a change.
>
> —Bob Waltz (Internet email)

Modern methods of textual restoration appear to promise a good degree of success when applying reasoned or rigorous eclecticism to the text of the New Testament. The resultant text created by modern eclectic methods, however, has an Achilles' heel that calls its entire methodology into question. Although modern eclectic methods apparently function well when evaluating readings within an isolated variant unit of text, the overall sequential linkage of readings from those separate variant units results in a running text that has absolutely *no* support from any known manuscript, version, or patristic writer within the entire period of historical textual transmission prior to the invention of printing. Even some single verses reflect this anomaly, and this stretches one's credulity far beyond what is even remotely possible, severely begging the question regarding what would in fact be most probable.

The original text of modern eclecticism thus becomes a phantom mirage with no real existence as soon as its readings are taken in sequence. The proffered original is a text whose distinctive pattern of agreement is far more likely *not* to reflect that lost autograph than to restore such. Is the autograph text of the New Testament therefore a mere mirage, or can something else be done to recover the original text of the New Testament with a greater degree of certainty? There is a solution, although it is not what most textual critics might prefer: the original text can be recovered primarily from the consensus agreement of the vast amount of manuscripts that comprise what is termed the "Byzantine Textform."[1]

Although the Byzantine Textform has generally been deprecated as late, conflationary, harmonizing, longer, and smoother, there remains a transmissional likelihood that this supposedly secondary Textform may in fact best exemplify the transmissional integrity of the New Testament text over the centuries. The present essay offers a brief description of the method and principles applied within a Byzantine-priority theory of textual restoration.[2]

The Essence of Byzantine Priority

Byzantine priority regards the perpetuation and preservation of the New Testament text as primarily a transmissional pro-

---

1. The term "Textform" as applied to the Byzantine text or text-type is a technical term that indicates the form of the text from which all other manuscripts, families, and text-types are presumed to have been derived.

2. The present essay is a summary of the paper prepared for the April 2000 symposium at Southeastern Seminary. This summary does not present a complete delineation of Byzantine-priority presuppositions, principles, evidences, reasoning, or application; nor does it include a detailed critique of various weaknesses within modern eclectic theory nor a response to specific criticisms and inaccurate claims that have been leveled against the Byzantine-priority theory. The original essay, with full documentation, may be read on the Internet in the electronic journal *TC: A Journal of Biblical Textual Criticism* (http://purl.org/TC/vol06/Robinson2001.html) and will also appear as an appendix in *The Greek New Testament according to the Byzantine Textform* (ed. M. A. Robinson and W. G. Pierpont; Boston: Chilton Book Publishing, forthcoming).

cess, affected always by the human element during the copying process. The theory requires one to view the history of the text as a "reasoned transmissionalism," carefully considering the effect of scribal habits and accidental and deliberate alteration of the text during the transmissional process. The historical-transmissional approach reflects to a good degree the concepts pioneered by WH. Westcott and Hort clearly recognized that textual criticism without a continually working history of transmission is impossible (thus indicting the modern eclectic method long before it existed). The Byzantine-priority theory, however, differs from that of WH by including the Byzantine Textform as a necessary primary component of the history of transmission and not as a Textform of secondary importance.

Modern reasoned or rigorous eclectics practice a methodology that treats variant readings as isolated entities separated into specific units. Within each unit, the supposedly "best" reading is determined on the basis of a number of valuable principles regarding both internal and external evidence. Since, however, these units remain methodologically isolated from one another, the manuscripts, versions, or fathers that support a reading in one variant unit are frequently at odds with the witnesses that support neighboring variant units. This is particularly seen when a continued sequence of units is examined and one observes the dwindling number of witnesses that support the progressing resultant text as each new unit is added. Such an examination, if continued, will imitate Alice's Cheshire cat— all visible support for the sequential text will utterly disappear, leaving only the smile of the proffered text as original.

Were such to occur only after a large number of variant units had been examined, perhaps the modern eclectic process could be excused. As it turns out, however, it usually takes only a small number of sequential variant units—and often only two such units within a single verse—to eliminate all semblance of actual manuscript support. This leaves a proferred "original" that over even short stretches of text has *no* demonstrable existence in any manuscript, version, or father during the entire scope of church history. Yet if one were to follow the aggregate testimony of *all* manuscripts over those same sequential variant units, one would find that a continual degree of support remains, and that support is found primarily among the Byzantine witnesses. The cause of such near-unanimity is not due to the great number of Byzantine witnesses (as some deridingly suggest), but rather to a *transmissional consistency* of text that becomes better defined as additional witnesses are added to the total. In fact, one could utilize a dozen or so non-Byzantine witnesses to create a "consensus text," and the result would be far closer to the Byzantine Textform than might be imagined.

The principle is simple: the more witnesses added to the pool, the more consistent the text becomes, regardless of the text-type of those witnesses. Since, however, the general tendency of such a consensus is to move closer to the Byzantine tradition, a theoretical presumption thereby exists that the Byzantine witnesses themselves may in fact present the strongest claim to autograph authenticity. These witnesses appear to preserve the basic transmissional form of the text far more accurately and consistently than witnesses of any other text-type.

A Byzantine-priority theory becomes necessary in view of the nature and results of modern eclectic practice. When all the "best" rules and manuscripts are utilized on a case-by-case basis merely to produce a sequential text with no legitimate manuscript, versional, or patristic support, both reasoned and thoroughgoing eclectics claim a text that lacks sufficient justification for either church or critical use. This forces one to inquire regarding *what* transmissional history could possibly be presumed for such an "original" text. One faces only a peculiar *mélange* of readings that are sporadically reflected in various manuscript and other witnesses. From such an eclectically determined original text, one must also accept a further proposition regarding its transmission from the autograph: although a text originally existed for each of the various New Testament books, soon after its creation it *totally* disappeared from transmissional lines and is no longer represented over even short stretches of text in any single existing manuscript. Such a proposition creates an anomaly unknown in other textual fields and precludes any hope of restoring the long-lost original, even by the most assiduous application of eclectic principles.

Modern eclecticism simply cannot demonstrate any transmissional descent from the text it puts forth as supposedly original. It is not merely that single verses have failed to leave traces in even one extant witness, but the problem increases geometrically as soon as a sequence of variants spans multiple verses. This continually leaves modern eclectic texts without valid support. In contrast, the Byzantine Textform at any point or over lengthy portions of text can demonstrate an overarching transmissional existence, not based upon merely a single manuscript or a small handful of manuscripts, but upon the broadest possible base of support. This phenomenon reflects transmissional reality as opposed to eclectic speculative hypotheses.

Principles for Restoring the Text

For the most part, the principles utilized in the practice and application of Byzantine-priority theory remain identical to those found in the standard text-critical handbooks regarding the eclectic methods. The issue is not the principles, but the total scope of their application; modern eclecticism sees only the individual variant units, while Byzantine-priority sees the sequential text as a whole.

Of all the modern eclectic principles, one principle that will not be used is preference for the shorter reading. It should be obvious that such a principle has an inherent bias that favors manuscripts containing a larger number of shorter readings, and for the most part those happen to be those witnesses that comprise the eclectically favored Alexandrian text-type. Since it has been determined from the examination of early papyri that scribes were, in fact, more prone to omit than to add material to their New Testament texts, a case readily can be made for the elimination of this principle, but without going to the other extreme of favoring the longer reading (a bias that would then favor the Western text). The remaining principles of New Testament textual criticism, assiduously applied, and keeping in mind the sequential resultant text, tend to support a predominantly Byzantine text. All that is required is to eliminate the anti-Byzantine bias that has prevailed for the last century and a half.

Another significant difference between Byzantine-priority and modern eclectic text-critical praxis is that the Byzantine position maintains a constant awareness of transmissional probabilities, particularly in regard to what is most likely to have resulted within transmissional history on the basis of the data we possess. Such an awareness includes recognition of transcriptional factors that have resulted in unintentional error, as well as various deliberate alterations of the text by scribes with "editorial" or recensional leanings.

The following list of working principles is divided into internal and external factors; all principles, however, need to function together in order for legitimate decisions to be made in regard to any variant reading. Since these principles for the most part reflect what is found in standard text-critical handbooks and also function as the working principles of most modern eclectics, little explanatory comment will be needed.

Principles of Internal Evidence

1. *The reading most likely to have given rise to all others within a variant unit is to be preferred.* Since variant readings by definition are those that deviate from the original text, it should be expected that such readings did not occur apart from some error or deliberate reasoning by a scribe. By careful examination of all possible causes for the creation of a variant reading, using internal, transcriptional, and transmissional evidence, it is possible in most instances to determine the reading most likely to have been original.

2. *The reading that would be more difficult as a scribal creation is to be preferred.* In this as well as in other internal principles, causes of error or deliberate alteration are attributable to known habits of scribes. These cases are *not*, however, reflective of the mass of scribes as a whole, despite claims made in the handbooks to such effect. In the present case, difficult readings created by individual scribes certainly exist, but these tend *not* to perpetuate to any significant degree within transmissional history. This can easily be demonstrated by careful examination of the available critical apparatuses. A corollary to this principle is that the more difficult reading *is* more strongly to be preferred when found in the transmissional *majority* of witnesses rather than when limited to a single witness or minority group. It is far more likely

that a minority of witnesses might possess a difficult reading merely due to error or individual scribal alteration as opposed to transmissional originality.

3. *Readings that conform to the known style, vocabulary, and syntax of the original author are to be preferred.* While this principle taken alone tends to characterize rigorous or thoroughgoing eclecticism, it must not be supposed that such has no validity within other text-critical methods. For the most part, it should be expected that within a given book, a New Testament author will generally conform to a certain style, syntax, and vocabulary, and that scribes in most cases would not be inclined to alter such authorial characteristics unless extremely rare words or improper grammar or syntax happened to appear.

4. *Readings that clearly harmonize or assimilate the wording of one passage to another are to be rejected.* While individual scribes often had a tendency to harmonize or assimilate wording, such generally occurred on a sporadic basis and is reflected primarily among individual manuscripts or small groups of manuscripts. There is little evidence to support any hypothesis of widespread scribal harmonization; for the most part scribes clearly can be shown *not* to have a harmonistic bent, else the Synoptic Gospel narratives would over time have become far more in harmony than they currently appear. The primary locus of harmonization and assimilation is within the immediate context (as opposed to remote parallels), and this in particular should be considered when evaluating variant readings.

5. *Readings reflecting common scribal piety or religiously motivated expansion or alteration tend to be secondary.* In general, such readings are readily discernible by their pious nature and lack of perpetuation among a significant number of manuscripts. One must not suppose, however, that all readings with some theological significance are thereby suspect merely because they reflect orthodox piety.

6. *The primary evaluation of readings should be based upon transcriptional probability.* Since manuscripts were trans-

mitted by hand, the cause of most variant readings must be sought in the probabilities regarding what a scribe would be likely to do (or not do) in any given case.

7. *Transcriptional error—rather than deliberate alteration— is more likely to be the ultimate source of many sensible variants.* Since scribal error has been shown to be far more common than deliberate alteration, the textual researcher should first ask whether some sort of scribal (transcriptional) error may have occasioned a given variant and also whether some of the remaining variants might reflect various attempts to repair the damage caused by such transcriptional error. Only after this has been done should inquiry be made into the likelihood of deliberate alteration by a given scribe, as well as to its perpetuation by later scribes.

8. *Neither the shorter nor longer reading is to be preferred.* While modern eclecticism assumes that scribes were more likely to expand rather than shorten the text in cases where an include/omit variation might occur, the opposite is the case. Accidental omission of single words or short phrases is now known to have occurred more frequently than deliberate expansion. Also, as mentioned earlier, the shorter-reading principle has a built-in bias that favors the Alexandrian text-type, since that text-type tends to be the shortest. Removal of this biased principle alters the results found in much of modern eclecticism. The optimal solution for New Testament textual criticism is to avoid adopting any principle that automatically dictates a decision geared to a specific text-type. Rather, *all* principles must work in harmony toward the goal of restoring the original text of the New Testament on a transmissional and scientific basis.

Principles of External Evidence

1. *The quantity of preserved evidence for the text of the New Testament precludes conjectural emendation.* The original text is presumed to have been preserved among the extant witnesses. This original is understood to be supported quantitatively and qualitatively within a dominant and

overarching Textform from which all competing minority text-types are presumed to have derived.

2. *Readings that appear sporadically within transmissional history are suspect.* This is the case, regardless of whether such readings are preserved in a single manuscript, version, or father or in a small group of witnesses.

3. *Variety of testimony is highly regarded.* A reading supported by various versions and fathers demonstrates a wider variety of support than a reading lacking such. Among Greek manuscripts, a reading shared among differing text-types is more strongly supported than that localized to a single text-type or family group.

4. *Wherever possible, the raw number of manuscripts should be intelligently reduced.* Many manuscripts can be demonstrated to have descended from a single archetype (e.g., the manuscripts comprising family 13, or the approximately 124 manuscripts of John in which the Greek Gospel text is interspersed with the commentary of Theophylact; these all stem from a single archetype and have very few significant variant readings among them).

5. *Manuscripts need to be weighed and not merely counted.* The Byzantine-priority position is not dependent upon the numerical majority that happens to support that Textform, but on the matter of what reflects transmissional reality and probability. The number of Byzantine manuscripts is not an ultimate criterion of authenticity, since there is no consistently united Byzantine text within the New Testament or even within any given New Testament book. In numerous places the manuscripts of the Byzantine Textform are nearly evenly divided among two or more variant readings. These divided readings clearly demonstrate that the Byzantine Textform is not homogenous and that there was no attempt or intent to enforce any standardization of that text.

6. *It is important to seek out readings with demonstrable antiquity.* The age of various witnesses demonstrates a datable existence for a reading (and, in the case of patristic quotations, a plausible locality) but not absolute antiquity. Two major disruptions affected transmis-

sional history: "copying revolutions" in which numerous ancient manuscripts were subjected to massive recopying efforts, resulting in the destruction of most previous exemplars.

   a. The first copying revolution occurred when Christianity was legitimized under Constantine and the church of the early fourth century moved from a persecuted minority to an approved entity with governmental sponsorship. The writing material began to shift from papyrus to vellum. As a result, one finds that most of our extant uncial manuscripts have *no* apparent stemmatic or genealogical ties to earlier extant vellum or papyrus witnesses. It can be presumed that most archetypes of our existing uncial manuscripts were early papyrus exemplars that no longer exist; they were either destroyed deliberately, discarded, or allowed to deteriorate following the conversion of their text to a sturdier vellum exemplar.

   b. The second copying revolution occurred in the ninth century when handwriting switched rapidly from uncial to minuscule script. The evidence suggests that uncial exemplars were destroyed after a minuscule copy had been made. Most surviving minuscules of the ninth through eleventh centuries appear to have no stemmatic ties to known extant uncial or papyrus exemplars; hence their genealogical independence and authoritative weight becomes significant, since these likely were copied from uncial exemplars no longer extant.

7. *The concept of a single best manuscript or small group of manuscripts is unlikely to have transmissional evidence in its favor.* Under a transmissional approach, what normally would be expected is the perpetuation of texts in a wide variety of manuscript formats. The likelihood that any individual manuscript in and by itself would reflect transmissional originality is not a consideration; rather, it is the aggregate testimony of the extant manuscript base that allows decisions to be made regarding originality of any given reading. The same principle holds for

small groups of manuscripts that by themselves are
more likely to reflect localized or regional transmissional variations rather than the original form of the
New Testament text; yet, when taken in conjunction
with other small groups from differing regions, their
aggregate testimony more likely reflects the autograph
than their mere local variety of text.

8. *Exclusively following the oldest manuscripts or witnesses
   is transmissionally flawed.* A variant reading found in a
   given witness (whether manuscript, version, or father) is
   guaranteed to be at least as old as the date of such a witness. Likewise, the pattern of readings found in a given
   witness, whether text-type-related or not, also dates
   from the same era of composition. A popular miscon-
   ception is that the earlier the witness, the earlier and
   more authoritative the text presented by that witness,
   merely because such a witness is chronologically closer
   to the time of autograph composition. It is known, however, that virtually all sensible variant readings came
   into existence during the tumultuous second century—
   the era of the "uncontrolled popular text"—and that
   what is reflected in all our extant manuscripts is a mixture of variant readings that date back into the obscurity
   of that era from which we have but scant textual information. Certainly, all existing witnesses utilized one or
   more exemplars that reflected an earlier form of text;
   but since a relatively recent manuscript may have been
   copied from a very ancient exemplar, the argument from
   age alone is fallacious. This supposition is further
   increased when one realizes that the two copying revolutions described above produced a negative impact regarding chronological date versus the antiquity of the text
   contained in any given witness.

9. *Transmissional considerations coupled with internal principles point to the Byzantine Textform as a leading force in
   the history of transmission.* The distinguishing feature of
   the Byzantine-priority method is its emphasis on a
   transmissional basis for understanding the history of the
   text and the restoration of that text by evaluating the
   readings of sequential variant units as primary compo-

nents of that text. This parallels manuscript transmission as found in secular literature. Further, given the massive quantity of evidence for the New Testament text as opposed to what exists for secular literature, the original text clearly can be expected to appear within an aggregate consensus of its manuscripts. Such a consensus text also finds additional support within the careful application of internal canons of criticism.

Balancing Internal and External Evidence

Given these criteria, the primary rules for balancing internal and external evidence become simple and are ordered in accord with known facts regarding scribal habits in the process of textual transmission. Allowing Byzantine-priority to function as a methodological principle, the rigorous application of this methodology according to the following sequence leads to valid conclusions established on a sound transmissional basis:

1. Evaluate readings with the intention of discovering antecedent transcriptional causes.
2. Consider readings in the light of possible intentional alteration.
3. Reevaluate readings within a variant unit from a transmissional-historical perspective in order to confirm or modify preliminary speculations.

Objections to and Support for the Byzantine-Priority Hypothesis

1. *There are no early Byzantine manuscripts prior to the fourth century.* The limited and localized nature of extant early manuscripts raises the possibility that presumptions regarding text-critical antiquity may be flawed. The two copying revolutions seriously affected the continuity of the transmissional stream. The localized text in Egypt is not likely to reflect what permeated the primary Greek-speaking portion of the empire (southern Italy, Greece, and modern Turkey), from which we have *no* manuscript, versional, or patristic data from before the

mid-fourth century. Yet the later existence and dominance of the Byzantine Textform in that region provides presumptive evidence supporting a similar dominance from previous times.

2. *The argument for the early existence of the Byzantine Textform rests on a stronger basis than the Synoptic Q-hypothesis.* While many New Testament scholars postulate the existence of a document Q to explain the apparent relationships that exist among the Synoptic Gospels, neither such a document nor even a fragment thereof has ever been found. The confidence with which advocates of Q maintain its existence, however, seems to be considerable. Yet while the Byzantine Textform cannot be shown to exist in any document preceding the fourth century, from that point onward manuscripts, versions, and patristic witnesses abound to testify to its existence. Such cannot be done with Q.

3. *The early existence of the Alexandrian text-type has been confirmed only within recent memory.* Until the discovery of $\mathfrak{P}^{75}$ in 1955, a relatively "pure" Alexandrian manuscript was unknown among the Egyptian papyri, and there was no proof that a text similar to that found in Codex Vaticanus existed prior to the fourth century. Yet now the early existence of the Alexandrian text-type is clearly established by $\mathfrak{P}^{75}$, even though the proof for such is only a half-century old. There is no *a priori* reason that precludes the discovery of an essentially Byzantine manuscript in the years to come, and, by analogy with the situation of $\mathfrak{P}^{75}$, such should not be eliminated as a possibility.

4. *Disruptions in the transmissional history supposedly eliminated the Byzantine predecessors and competitors.*

    a. *The Diocletian or other persecutions.* Persecutions were not selective in their textual targets. Any manuscripts surrendered and destroyed would reflect the general proportion of existing manuscripts in a given region regardless of text-type; so also would the manuscripts that survived.

    b. *The Islamic conquest.* Especially in the earliest times, Islam was not as totally destructive to Christianity or the New Testament manuscripts as has been claimed. Monasteries and the Coptic church continued to survive and maintain literary activity under Islam. Communication and travel were maintained between churches and monasteries in Islamic regions and the Byzantine East.

c. *The popularity and influence of Chrysostom.* Chrysostom used a near-Byzantine text while in Constantinople. Yet there is no evidence that the church ever followed closely or adopted the New Testament text of any father, regardless of his preaching or writing reputation. There is no historical record of any imposition of control upon the New Testament text or its scribes and manuscripts by decree of either church or empire.

d. *The Byzantine Textform supposedly can be understood as the result of a process.* In theory, such a process over the centuries steadily moved away from the original form of the text in the interest of smoothness, harmonization, and grammatical and other "improvements." The primary problem with the process model lies in explaining how such a process could function given the exigencies of transmission and location apart from decree or collusion. A properly nuanced process view recognizes various factors involved in the transmissional process: (a) a tendency toward regional deviation into localized forms over the centuries; and (b) the transcriptional production of various subtypes within any localized, recensional, or dominant text-type. Apart from formal imposition of controls, the end result of any transmissional process is a text *diverging* continually from the parent text-type, contrary to the presuppositions of modern eclecticism.

Concluding Observations

Byzantine-priority theory provides a compelling and logical perspective. This theory can stand on its own merits in the quest toward the goal of establishing the original text of the New Testament, since it attempts to explain the evidential data preserved. Such a theory has a methodological consistency that cannot be demonstrated among the various modern eclectic alternatives. Apart from a transmissionally oriented base, any claims to approach and establish an authoritative form of the original text of the New Testament by a purely eclectic method will consistently fall short.

For the past century, modern eclecticism has functioned without an integrated history of textual transmission. Its resultant text has no root in any single document, group of documents, or text-type—and this is but an unfortunate by-product of its self-imposed methodology. Thoroughgoing eclecticism divorces itself from external criteria, while reasoned eclecticism attempts to strike a balance between internal and external considerations. Yet both systems fail precisely at the point of transmissional history, producing a resultant text that reflects a piecemeal assemblage created from disparate variant units otherwise unrelated to each other.

It is precisely at this point that the Byzantine-priority theory does *not* fail, but instead offers a transmissionally legitimate form of resultant text. In contrast, modern text-critical thought tends to move steadily away from the concept of "original" text, having become more interested in questionable speculations such as whether heterodox scribes perhaps treated the text more reliably than did the orthodox. Overall, modern eclecticism leaves an atmosphere of general uncertainty and despair regarding the possible recovery of the original text of the New Testament; its practitioners are no longer certain that the original text can be recovered or whether any concept of an original text can be maintained.

In contrast, the Byzantine-priority theory offers a clear practical alternative to current subjectivity and the often pessimistic suppositions that characterize modern eclectic theory. It reflects a legitimate text-critical method that aims properly at the restoration of the best attainable original text of the New Testament by the best available means.

5

RESPONSE

Moisés Silva

As a rule, I welcome with open arms any kind of invitation to be a respondent. If you are asked to read a paper, that's a lot of work and grief. Not only do you have to break your neck researching the material and polishing your writing so that it makes sense, but you are also in the hot seat. As a respondent, on the other hand, you merely need to read the papers being presented and start pontificating. And if anyone has the poor taste to raise a question or objection, you can easily deflect the criticism to the main speakers!

I said, "As a rule. . . ." It's really a matter of statistical probability—a subject that will occupy us again momentarily. In this particular case, unfortunately, my strategy backfired a bit, for textual criticism is really a complicated problem. But then again, maybe that only works in my favor. After all, no one could reasonably expect me to give an adequate response to so many complicated ideas.

All four presenters at the April 2000 symposium at Southeastern Seminary placed us in their debt by helping us examine our assumptions and rethink our commitments. During the past several decades, Eldon Epp has had no peer in what we may call the history of ideas applied to New Testament textual criticism. Not merely his knowledge of the development of this field, but more important, the incisiveness with which he has evaluated its methods, makes his work almost unique in our discipline. Reading his clear analyses—including the present essay—always feels like a breath of fresh air.

Michael Holmes is one of the most prominent current defenders of what we may call mainstream textual criticism, and his essay tells you why: he has given a great deal of attention to questions of principle and method, but not in isolation from the actual work of textual analysis.

J. K. Elliott, a tireless scholar whose output in our field is exceptional, has given us a kinder, gentler brand of so-called thoroughgoing eclecticism, and his effort to show the points of contact between his approach and the mainstream method is warmly appreciated.

Finally, Maurice Robinson has with characteristic erudition challenged our complacency. Since I personally worry a great deal about the atomistic tendencies of biblical scholarship, I am especially grateful for his critique of any method that reaches decisions on individual variants without sufficient attention to the larger picture.

I was not, however, invited to the symposium to say nice things about our speakers, and so I move on to the real business.

First of all, though, let me disabuse you of any thoughts that I am an impartial and objective party in the dispute. The truth is that I am an unrepentant and unshaken Hortian. Keep in mind that what Hort did—in collaboration with Westcott and, less directly, Lightfoot—was primarily to *synthesize* and logically *articulate* nineteenth-century text-critical scholarship, which was itself the culmination of intensive work tracing its lineage back to Bengel in the eighteenth century, Bentley in the seventeenth century, and Erasmus in the sixteenth century. Yes, Erasmus, because even the creator of what would be later known as the *textus receptus* was absolutely committed to the very principles that lie at the foundation of WH's accomplishments.

One of the oddest curiosities in the modern controversy is the common perception of Hort as an innovator. In fact, there is precious little in the *substance* of his work that can be accurately described as original—and what can be thus described lies pretty much at the periphery and does not significantly affect the main thesis. But his work does indeed display brilliant originality in the *organization and exposition* of the subject matter. Having had considerable experience as a botanist, Hort applied his scientific training and extraordinary analytical powers to the study of textual variation. His starting point was the achievements of previous scholars, prominently the work of Bengel and Griesbach, but closer to him in time the advances made by Lachmann, Tischendorf, and Tregelles.

Hort's job was to gather all the relevant data, to restructure the material, and to fill in the blanks, which meant primarily making explicit what until then was only implicit, though, of course, at some points new research and conceptualization were necessary. Once the whole argument had been constructed, the result was quite simply a thing of beauty. Even a look at the detailed table of contents of WH's introduction tells you that you are dealing with a remarkable mind. It is no wonder that even Hort's opponent Scrivener said of this work: "Never was a cause, good or bad in itself, set off with higher ability and persuasive power."[1]

Indeed, it is the *persuasiveness* of Hort's argumentation that has made his work appear innovative to some observers. Here for the first time the arguments were laid out in a complete and systematic fashion, with all the implications drawn out (both theoretically and practically, since it included the publication of a critical text). What was this? A new teaching—and with authority? (cf. Mark 1:27) No. In all essential points—the validity of the text-critical canons, the superiority of ancient documents, the importance of textual groupings, and the relatively late char-

1. F. H. A. Scrivener, *A Plain Introduction to the Criticism of the New Testament* (London: Bell, 1894), 2:242. On 2:296 he tells us what his experience was; the more he read WH's introduction, "the more it grows upon our esteem for fulness of learning, for patience of research, for keenness of intellectual powers, and especially for a certain marvellous readiness in accounting after some fashion for every new phenomenon which occurs, however apparently adverse to the acceptance of his own theory."

acter of the Majority text—Hort was merely adopting views that had been widely accepted by specialists for several generations.

I don't believe that Hort was perfect (I reserve that term for Lightfoot), nor do I want to suggest that New Testament textual criticism has made no progress since WH. Yet nearly every time I go back to Hort's introduction I find that he had quite effectively anticipated many of the challenges and objections that we continue to hear in our day, maybe even in this volume of essays.

Consider, for example, the role of internal evidence, especially questions about intrinsic probability, which Elliott regards as having preeminent importance. A fair reading of WH's introduction as a whole demonstrates that Hort attached extraordinary weight to matters of internal evidence while at the same time recognizing the true relationship between it and external evidence. It is well known that Hort initially assigned relative value to the manuscripts on the basis of internal evidence of readings. In fact, some people actually suggest that Hort was guilty of invalid circular reasoning, because he then turned around and used those manuscripts to make decisions on individual readings. That's quite a silly accusation, of course. Is there any scientific field where some such process ("spiral" would be a better metaphor) is not routinely practiced?[2]

Be that as it may, the point is that the use of internal evidence is bedrock material in Hort's approach. We must not, however, forget the language that he used to describe the use of this evidence: he called it "the most rudimentary form of criticism" (WH 2:19). The term *rudimentary* speaks volumes. It tells you on the one hand that unless you have that, you can't go anywhere else—it is absolutely basic. But it also tells you that if that's all you have, there's not much you can do with it.

Part of the problem is that the analysis of internal evidence involves examining variants "independently" (WH 2:19). But even

---

2. Some years ago in one of my classes, a student who had begun to study theology after a career in science, upon hearing this objection to Hort's method, began to laugh. It was quite evident to him that Hort was following standard scientific procedure (briefly described in WH 2:32–35). Curiously, Elliott proposes the same method: "But what I am conceding is that by examining without prejudice the readings in all manuscripts we may at a later stage reach decisions about the relative worthiness of particular witnesses to support, perhaps even singly, the original text" (p. 123 above).

more problematic is the ambiguity inherent at this stage of the process. This is especially true of intrinsic probability: while in some cases the arguments attain great force, "the uncertainty of the decision in ordinary cases is shown by the great diversity of judgement which is actually found to exist. . . . Equally competent critics often arrive at contradictory conclusions as to the same variations" (WH 2:21).[3] We may not like the term *subjective* as a description of thoroughgoing eclecticism, but the fact is that such an approach—even in the gentler version offered by Elliott—does not provide a means of moving beyond this basic impasse.

With regard to transcriptional probability, and in particular the canon of the shorter reading, I need to play the part of Athanasius *contra mundum*. It is, of course, true that if *all* we say is that the shorter reading is to be preferred, that is patently untrue in numerous cases, as Royse and others have shown. But I think it is a slander on our text-critical forefathers to even suggest that they had such a naive understanding of the facts. Considering that Griesbach's classic formulation of this canon is readily accessible in English,[4] there is no excuse for any student to misuse it. Griesbach not only lists the specific situations in which the shorter reading is to be preferred; he also provides an even longer list of situations in which "the longer reading is to be preferred to the shorter." Indeed, the vast majority of counterexamples in the papyri given by Royse are covered by Griesbach's qualifications. Even Scrivener, for all his skepticism regarding the application of this canon, acknowledged that it was true in principle.[5]

3. A striking example of the danger is afforded by Luke 2:14, where the genitive εὐδοκίας is almost universally accepted by Lukan scholars in our day. Scrivener (*Plain Introduction*, 2:344) thought that such a reading mars the threefold stanza, and so he considered this variation the most prominent case where "solid reason and pure taste revolt against the iron yoke of ancient authorities." And when Elliott uses language like "my own impression is . . ." (p. 111 above), it is difficult not to think of the term *subjective*.

4. B. M. Metzger, *The Text of the New Testament: Its Transmission, Corruption, and Restoration* (3d ed.; New York: Oxford University Press, 1992), 120.

5. Serivener, *Plain Introduction*, 2:249–50. At any rate, Hort quite clearly understood that the canons are no more than generalizations that single out "proclivities of average copyists" (WH 2:23), that is, "judgements founded on previous investigation of the various general characteristics of those readings which can with moral certainty be assumed to have been introduced by scribes" (WH 2:24).

In this connection, I'd like to make a comment regarding Housman's dog, mentioned by Holmes. I have already alluded to Hort's scientific training and the impact of that training on his work. It is evident that when he spoke of "probability"—and in particular "transcriptional probability"—he was using the term not in its popular, casual sense, but in a more sophisticated way, that is, the drawing of inferences based on carefully gathered statistical data. Now some practitioners of our discipline resist any talk that sounds mathematical. And while I have great admiration for both Housman's text-critical work and his cogitations on the subject, we need to make a distinction between those instances when he is communicating genuine insights and those times when he is, well, venting.

I suggest that his remark about dogs and fleas belongs in the latter category. Think of a life-insurance company that spends considerable time and effort gathering statistical data on death rates and applying mathematical formulas to the data in order to draw dependable actuarial tables. Now imagine that one of the executives—a successful entrepreneur with a real knack for making business decisions—objects to this research: "All of this data doesn't tell me when any one specific individual is going to die, so the information is useless. Besides, constructing mathematical tables does not conform to canine behavior!" I love dogs (assuming other people are taking care of them), but I have some misgivings about patterning my professional life after them. The reason dogs don't use probability theory is that they are *brute* beasts. If they could use it, I guarantee you that they would catch more fleas.[6]

I could expand on this subject, but we need to move on to external evidence. Robinson is troubled by the fact that if we take not one or two individual variations but a stretch of text, our modern critical editions do not correspond exactly to any one manuscript, let alone a textual tradition. As I mentioned at the beginning, we are indebted to Robinson for reminding us that we cannot merrily go around making individual decisions on

6. Of course, Housman's concern was to emphasize, if we may use the common language, that textual criticism is an art as well as a science, in the sense that you cannot apply rules to it mechanically. But how much of genuine science works in such a fashion anyway? Is anyone prepared to say that Einstein's relativity principle is science without art? The dichotomy is a false one.

variants without taking a step back and asking whether the picture as a whole coheres. But when a reconstructed text looks like a mishmash from various witnesses, does that necessarily indicate a defect in our method?

Suppose that the following had taken place during the course of the symposium: As the speakers are presenting their papers, I jot down a couple of sentences, indicating a possible solution to one of the text-critical problems being raised. Suppose further that Holmes happens to see it and decides to copy it, except that he leaves out a definite article in the first sentence. He then hands it to Robinson, who also copies it and who coincidentally leaves out the same definite article because it does not affect the meaning. Elliott too copies the text, but changes my *-or* endings into the British spelling *-our* and makes other orthographic adjustments. Finally, Epp gets hold of the piece of paper and also copies it. His copy is flawless—in fact, it is better than the original, since he believes that the original is not quite as useful as what later people do with it. In particular, he realizes that I have allowed my Spanish substratum to alter an English idiom, and so he corrects it.

Two months later, Robinson shows his copy of my text to David Black, who is so impressed by its brilliance that he copies it, making an additional scribal alteration. He then tells his students to make their own copies—and they had better make no mistakes in the transcription because they are required to memorize it. As a result, thirty virtually identical manuscripts (except for punctuation or capitalization) are produced.

Within a year, my solution to the problem becomes canonical, and Bruce Metzger is asked to publish the *editio princeps*. He calls me, hoping that I can produce the autograph, but I have since lost the original precious piece of paper. Undaunted, Metzger recovers the copies made by the other essayists and compares them to the Majority text. He immediately recognizes the omission of the definite article as a careless scribal mistake, the *-our* endings as a stylistic recension, and the proper English idiom as a smoothing of the more difficult reading. He further finds that the distinctive pattern of the Majority text cannot be traced back to an ancient stage, so he sets it aside.

Metzger finally reconstructs the text and publishes a critical, eclectic edition. His text as a sequence is not attested in any one witness and so looks like a mishmash. But guess what—it is identical to the original! In fact, the more you reflect on it the more you realize that the *appearance* of mishmash is exactly what you would expect unless you have the prior conviction that one particular witness or group of witnesses has not been susceptible to normal scribal changes. But if every copyist is vulnerable to such changes and thus is fallible, we should hardly be surprised to notice a lack of correspondence between a properly reconstructed text and the surviving witnesses.

This lack of complete correspondence, however, needs to be distinguished from quite a different issue, namely, the lack of early evidence for the pattern of readings characterizing the Majority text. In this latter instance we ask what makes a particular textual tradition recognizable. Now when we look at the text attested in the majority of New Testament manuscripts and identify its distinctive configuration, we cannot but be impressed by the silence of the early historical record.

In Galatians, for example, what makes the Majority text distinctive is, first, the consistent use of the name *Peter* instead of *Cephas*[7] and the presence of certain words and phrases not found elsewhere.[8] Although most of these readings, considered individually, are attested in early witnesses, the configuration as such is not found in any Greek manuscript prior to the ninth century (the ninth-century uncials Ψ and 0278 agree with this basic configuration better than 80%). In fact, the pre-ninth-century Greek manuscript that comes closest to this configuration is Codex D, which supports seven of the fifteen readings in question, less than 50%.[9] And as is well known, no witness of any kind prior to the fourth century can be shown to reflect a text with such a pattern of readings. We have significant second- and third-century evidence from Gaul (Irenaeus), Italy and North

---

7. See 1:18; 2:11, 14. The name *Peter* is uncontested in 2:7–8. The Majority text supports *Cephas* only in 2:9.

8. Including "for" in 1:10b; "not to disobey the truth" in 3:1; "to/for Christ" in 3:17; "and" in 3:29; "of God through Christ" (versus simply "through God") in 4:7; "was" in 4:15; "all" in 4:26; "adultery" in 5:19; "murders" in 5:21; "and" in 5:21b; "in Christ Jesus" in 6:15; "Lord" in 6:17.

9. Three additional readings are supported by late correctors of D. Chrysostom, whose fourth-century text may be regarded as the earliest attested expression of the Majority text, supports maybe 75% of the readings.

Africa (Old Latin, Tertullian), Egypt (papyri, Clement), Palestine (Origen), and Syria (Old Syriac), and nowhere is the Majority-text configuration attested.

Of course, one can always come up with possible scenarios to account for lack of evidence (e.g., "all the good manuscripts were worn out from use"), but some of us may be forgiven if we are unable to get past this fundamental problem.

In conclusion, I would like to affirm—not only with Hort, but with practically all students of ancient documents—that the recovery of the original text (i.e., the text in its initial form, prior to the alterations produced in the copying process) remains the primary task of textual criticism. Of course, it is not the only task. The study of early textual variation for its own sake is both a fascinating and a most profitable exercise. And it is also true that we have sometimes been sloppy in our use of the term *original text*. But neither these truths nor the admittedly great difficulties involved in recovering the autographic words can be allowed to dissolve the concept of an original text. Nor do I find it helpful when David Parker, for example, sanctifies his proposals by a theological appeal to a divinely inspired textual diversity—indeed, textual confusion and contradiction—that is supposed to be of greater spiritual value than apostolic authority.

But even apart from that, for us to retreat from the traditional task of textual criticism is equivalent to shooting ourselves in the foot. And my exhibit A is Bart Ehrman's brilliant monograph *The Orthodox Corruption of Scripture*, which I consider one of the most significant contemporary works on biblical scholarship. Although this book is appealed to in support of blurring the notion of an original text, there is hardly a page in that book that does not in fact mention such a text or assume its accessibility. "Why is such-and-such a reading in Mark a later corruption and not original? Because Mark (authorial intent!) would not likely have said such a thing." Indeed, Ehrman's book is unimaginable unless he can identify an initial form of the text that can be differentiated from a later alteration.

Undeniably, some textual problems (the divorce sayings, for example) in our present state of knowledge may prove intractable. No one has claimed that in New Testament textual criticism—any more than in any other field of knowledge—we will reach a solution to every problem. But we cannot allow the exceptional to determine our total course of action. Let us not forget that the distinctive challenges in our field are actually the result of enormous quantities of data (unavailable for other documents whose originality we take for granted!) and of extraordinary scholarly advances. Encouraged by this reality, we have plenty of good reasons to press on.

SUBJECT INDEX

SCRIPTURE INDEX

Made in the USA
Lexington, KY
08 August 2013